Advance praise for
Quality Makes Money

"There are several aspects of this book that are refreshing and different. The two that will have the most resonance with practitioners are the inextricable link between quality and leadership, and viewing quality as a comprehensive capability. It's a tall order, but as the examples illustrate, one that is essential to producing enduring improvement in performance."

Vinita Bali
CEO
Britannia Industries Ltd.
Bangalore, India

"Quality = Leadership = shareholder and stakeholder return. *Quality Makes Money* successfully demonstrates through an effective case study that quality is a holistic process which must be driven by senior management. This drive must be sustained and committed and is synonymous with achieving revenue growth, profitability, and client satisfaction. The authors prove that your sustained quality initiative is good for business and that's the primary reason for doing it."

Martin Searle
General Manager, Professional Services
SAI-Global

"Townsend and Gebhardt do a great job of introducing their Complete Quality Process to us, which takes into account not only the tools available to analyze, institute, measure, and record quality practices, but also the environment in which these tools are consistently and enthusiastically applied. They give great examples and follow up with a nice set of practice problems. They provide success stories and pitfalls to be avoided from their real working environment and breadth of experience. Most importantly, they emphasize and show the way for 100 percent involvement of the people in our workplaces. It is obvious that sustainability only derives from participation of the employees—leaders who understand that improvement really comes from the bottom up, and that procedure-by-procedure, paper-by-paper, person-by-person, load-by-load, part-by-part, and day-by-day, improvements converge to yield sustainable gains.

There is a powerful statement of the Samurai code: Do not make anything useless. This book captures this vision by using uncomplicated terminology, explaining the steps that should be taken in a simple way, and including the important issue of how to save money with quality practices. This very well-written book's simplified approaches and methods can be easily applied to any organization, no matter what field you may be in. I strongly believe it is a valuable guide for working and leading in the twenty-first century. I recommend this book for everyone in business and find it particularly essential for leaders, managers, quality professionals, and business owners."

Dr. Seval Akgün, MD, PhD
Professor, Baskent University, Ankara, Turkey
Chief Quality Officer for Baskent University Hospital Network

"As Pat Townsend and Joan Gebhardt point out in their new book, *Quality Makes Money*, you need to do it all . . . nobody hires a one-ball juggler! There is a need for complete commitment, or what the authors call the Complete Quality Process. That includes the most crucial aspect: implementation.

There is no lack of literature on quality with advice on what to do. But have services really become better? In this respect, *Quality Makes Money* stands out. The authors have successfully implemented quality in organizations and followed it to the bottom line. They know both the book smarts and the street smarts. On top of that they write well and are direct and exciting to read. They demand disciplined work but also creativity and courage to swim against the mainstream. And they do it based on real-world observation and experience of what works and what doesn't."

Dr. Evert Gummesson
Professor of Service Management
Stockholm University School of Business, Sweden
Recipient of the American Marketing Association's Award
for Leadership in the Service Field
Author of *Total Relationship Marketing* and *Many-to-Many Marketing*

"Townsend and Gebhardt's latest work gives us a unique case study—a guided tour through a culture-based performance improvement experiment. Interestingly, this experiment is being conducted at a time when many organizations have turned to tool-driven initiatives, often ones that are variants of initiatives that have lost some luster under their former names. This work builds upon the authors' observations and experiences over more than two decades and upon their keen and sensitive grasp of how the world works for those who actually do the tasks that might need to be improved. The authors develop and clearly illustrate the essential principles of what they call a Complete Quality Process.

Although the authors' main focus is on the people and cultural dimensions of organizational performance, they don't neglect the stern realities that such performance creates in the boardroom. Their discussion of the economic case for quality provides the reader with a critical bridge between the performance gains that individuals 'see' and the net performance gains that senior leaders dare not do without. Their bridge is constructed from several key anchors and pillars: savings per employee, types of savings, trends in savings, uses of savings, steep decrease in employee turnover, and dramatic improvement in aggregate productivity. This provides readers with key insights into the always puzzling distinction (and dynamic tension) between quality and productivity.

The book should be read by those faced with performance challenges, by students of organizational behavior, and by those doing postmortems of failed initiatives. This easily read work should provide the reader with numerous insights into the dynamics of performance in knowledge work and office environments—ones where motivation is critical to success, and ones in which tool-driven and jargon-based approaches often fail to take root. Townsend and Gebhardt help us to see the challenge through what they call an emotional/rational commitment—which translates into performance for all stakeholders."

Dr. Curt W. Reimann
Senior Scientist Emeritus and Director (1987–1995)
Malcolm Baldrige National Quality Award
National Institute of Standards and Technology

Quality Makes Money

Pat Townsend
and Joan Gebhardt

ASQ Quality Press
Milwaukee, Wisconsin

American Society for Quality, Quality Press, Milwaukee 53203
© 2006 by American Society for Quality
All rights reserved. Published 2005
Printed in the United States of America

12 11 10 09 08 07 06   5 4 3 2 1

Library of Congress Cataloging-in-Publication Data

Townsend, Patrick L.
  Quality makes money / Pat Townsend.
    p. cm.
  Includes bibliographical references and index.
  ISBN 0-87389-660-2 (alk. paper)
  1. Total quality management.   2. Total quality control.   I. Title.

  HD62.15.T694 2005
  658.4'013--dc22

2005011261

Publisher: William A. Tony
Acquisitions Editor: Annemieke Hytinen
Project Editor: Paul O'Mara
Production Administrator: Randall Benson

ASQ Mission: The American Society for Quality advances individual, organizational, and community excellence worldwide through learning, quality improvement, and knowledge exchange.

Attention Bookstores, Wholesalers, Schools, and Corporations: ASQ Quality Press books, videotapes, audiotapes, and software are available at quantity discounts with bulk purchases for business, educational, or instructional use. For information, please contact ASQ Quality Press at 800-248-1946, or write to ASQ Quality Press, P.O. Box 3005, Milwaukee, WI 53201-3005.

To place orders or to request a free copy of the ASQ Quality Press Publications Catalog, including ASQ membership information, call 800-248-1946. Visit our Web site at www.asq.org or http://qualitypress.asq.org.

Quality Press
600 N. Plankinton Avenue
Milwaukee, Wisconsin 53203
Call toll free 800-248-1946
Fax 414-272-1734
www.asq.org
http://qualitypress.asq.org
http://standardsgroup.asq.org
E-mail: authors@asq.org

♾ Printed on acid-free paper

To John Fynn and Candace Whelan

Table of Contents

Introduction . . . .   *xiii*

Chapter 1   **A Complete Quality Process** **1**

Maybe Some Other Time   2
Simple, but Difficult   5

Chapter 2   **The Economic Case for Quality** **7**

Consumer Power   8
Capacity for Work   10
Show Me the Money   12
A Case Study of Profit   14
Top Management Commitment   17

Chapter 3   **Active Commitment at the Top** **19**

Putting a Face on Quality   19
A Case Study in Top Management
        Commitment   23
Sustaining Commitment at the Top   29

Chapter 4   **Leading with Confidence** **33**

Emotional/Rational Commitment   35
The Implications of Trust   36
Pushing Authority Down   38
A Crash Course in Leadership   41
Setting the Example   43
The PEET Program   45
A Case Study in Leadership   46

Chapter 5	**The Ins and Outs of Participation**	**49**
	Too Ambitious for Us	51
	Beware the Quality Purists	53
	A Case Study in Participation	55
	Quality Teams at the Insurance Center	60
	Doing Things Right vs. Doing Right Things	63
	Gaining Momentum	64
	Changing the Process	66
Chapter 6	**Investing in the Future**	**71**
	Getting Oriented	72
	Addendum to Leadership	75
	It Takes Teamwork	76
	A Word on Outside Vendors	78
	Quality Training versus Job Training	79
	Sad, but True	80
Chapter 7	**Progress and Possibilities**	**83**
	A Survey of Measurement	86
	It's Not for Me	90
	Uniquely CQP	91
	Measuring Success	94
Chapter 8	**Celebrate Good Times!**	**97**
	The Problem—and Challenge	101
	Impact on Senior Management	102
	And . . . the Bottom Line	103
	Celebrations	103
	Punny, Isn't It?	105
Chapter 9	**As I Was Saying**	**107**
	Listening Down	108
	Transmission and Reception	109
	Introducing Quality	111
	What's in It for Me?	112
	An Invitation to Change	116
	Pam Walsh's "Unofficial Tips to Quality"	116
	We Haven't Got Time	118

Broadcasting an Update 119
Mission, Quality, and Pie-in-the-Face? 120
What Exactly Is a Culture Shift? 121

Chapter 10   Now What? **123**

Appendix A   *The Spirit of Quality in America by Pat*
               Townsend 125

Appendix B   *Love and Leadership by Pat Townsend* 129

Appendix C   *The Anatomy of a Dictaphone by*
               Lillian S. Murphy 135

References 141

Index 143

About the Authors 151

Introduction

It has been more than a dozen years since my co-author and partner Joan Gebhardt and I last wrote a book specifically about quality. The intervening period left us with strong opinions about the best way for an organization to become the quality alternative in any field, and we are writing this book to describe some of what we experienced.

By the time our last book on quality was published (1992), we had moved away from having "real jobs" and were in the business of giving speeches about quality (me) and conducting workshops on how to define and implement a quality process (us). Thanks to our travels throughout the United States and several countries in Europe, Asia, and South America, we had a ringside seat for watching the development and partial demise of the American Quality Revolution, as well as like efforts in several nations. During this period, we wrote extensively on the topics of leadership, recognition, and institutional learning—aspects of quality that we wanted to examine more closely.

Neither then nor now can I claim that we represent mainstream thinking in the quality field. My first experience with quality began before there were consultants who tied the words *service* and *quality* together. As a result, a process I helped initiate in the years 1983–1984 at the Paul Revere Insurance Group was forced to go with what seemed obvious, rather than with what later passed for group/experiential knowledge.

In the early-to-mid 1980s, we at Paul Revere involved every single employee in the effort to improve every aspect of the organization, and we acted on the belief that leadership and quality were two inexorably intertwined concepts. Imagine my partner's and my surprise when both positions (and several others that will be addressed in the chapters to come) turned out in the mid-to-late 1990s to be minority views! The publisher of our first book on quality even had us remove a chapter on leadership because its editorial board could see no connection between the two disciplines.

As my partner and I learned more about how to ensure continual improvement in an organization, so did the nation. There was one extremely positive development in 1987: the definition and introduction of the Malcolm Baldrige National Quality Award. This award is, without question, the best thing that has happened to American business in the last 100 years. But once you exclude those folks willing to put in the hard work needed to conform to the Baldrige criteria (a distinct and generally very successful minority), progress in the world of quality has been uneven at best. As an indication of the inconsistency of results, consider that early in the twenty-first century there is an ongoing search for a new word, a word other than "quality," to act as the code word for all of the activity that used to fall under the quality banner.

Why the need for a new word or phrase? (The voting seems to be leaning toward "performance excellence" or "continual improvement"; "added value" seems to have fallen by the wayside.) The main reason is the bastardization of the word "quality" by a large number of management fads *du jour*. While I roamed the speakers circuit, I watched as various consultants and companies claimed to have discovered the shortcut to quality. Reengineering specialists said it took an emphasis on process analysis, rooting out weaknesses and duplication. Statisticians said that a single-minded focus on SPC (statistical process control) was the answer. Leadership advocates said that senior executive teams could take care of everything by following their (the advocates') particular set of principles. Among other supposed silver bullets were TQM (Total Quality Management—usually anything but), Kaizen, ISO, lean, and Six Sigma. But none of these high visibility tools worked for any length of time, at least not in isolation, and some (especially reengineering) did real damage.

Seeing all of these cure-alls rise and fade simply reinforced our thinking that what had been done in the early-to-mid 1980s at Paul Revere had been really remarkable—in large part because it pretty much incorporated all of these ideas into one process. Still, thinking about quality and creating quality are two different things. The timing was right when, after being on the speakers circuit for a dozen years, I received a phone call from an insurance company just outside of Fort Worth. Their question—or challenge—was, essentially, "You've been telling lots of people how to do this quality/leadership thing . . . care to do it here?"

This was an opportunity to try out ideas that we had been refining ever since that initial success at the Paul Revere Insurance Group in the years 1983–1988. The resulting experience is the source of most of the examples in this book. I have to say, on a personal level (that is, after all, one of the reasons for writing an introduction: to be able to say things on a personal level) that it has been wonderfully satisfying to verify that virtually everything we advised in all of those speeches, articles, and workshops really can be done—and truly does have an impressive, positive impact.

This book describes a pragmatic set of steps that make it possible for an organization of any type to engage every person on their payroll in the continual effort to improve everything the company does. To use one of the trendy words of the early twenty-first century, our intention is to *reenergize* the quality revolution in the United States by giving organizations a realistic option for tapping into the talent already on their payrolls. The book presents not only logical theory, but also a real-life, full-scale success story as a model. Paying heed to its lessons can enable organizations of all types to improve whatever it is they do and see a positive impact on the bottom line.

And one further note . . . getting back into the business of writing a book has been made far easier than I remembered it being by folks who have been wonderfully generous with their time and talent—and added some humor besides. They are Paul O'Mara (Project Editor) and Annemieke Hytinen (Acquisitions Editor) of the American Society for Quality and the staff of Kinetic Publishing Services. Joan and I are very grateful for their help, support, and professionalism.

Pat Townsend

1 A Complete Quality Process

The American Quality Revolution got rolling in the mid-to-late 1980s in large part because of the thinking and charismatic leadership of three men: Dr. W. Edwards Deming, Dr. Joseph Juran, and Dr. Tom Peters. Deming and Juran (and other pioneers such as Dr. Armand Feigenbaum) gave the movement its brain; Peters gave it its heart by inspiring American business leaders to believe that they, too, could improve quality and that they could excel. Subsequent research examined methodologies for defining, implementing, and maintaining ways to take advantage of the principles and practices conceived and taught by Deming and Juran while at the same time appealing to and enlisting the hearts and wills of individuals, as Peters demonstrated it is possible to do. A Complete Quality Process (CQP), the topic of this book, strikes that balance.

CQP takes into account not only the tools available to analyze, institute, measure, and record quality practices, but also the environment in which these tools are consistently and enthusiastically applied. How does it differ from past approaches, quality fads that enjoyed a brief vogue for improving quality before their reputations tarnished? The key is the C in CQP: complete. CQP contrasts sharply with efforts that address only one specific portion of the total range of quality challenges and that don't come close to involving (in the sense of asking for ideas and input and sharing decision-making capabilities) 100 percent of the people on the payroll. The touchstones are balance and perseverance. The methodology allows for—and, in fact, encourages—the appropriate use of any quality tool, while underscoring the importance of having the will to use those tools. It's sustainable, and best of all, it doesn't take a lot of time to get it up and running.

A CQP consists of seven components that, when incorporated into a balanced process, make it possible for an organization to become

1

a consistent provider of quality information, services, and/or products while continuing to improve. It begins with top management commitment, includes leadership, makes 100 percent employee involvement (with a structure) a source of ideas, and supports the whole with measurement, training, recognition, and communications. Organizations cannot avoid addressing any of these issues—even when they do so by default—and what CQP does is address them in the simplest yet most comprehensive manner consistent with good quality practices.

Though 100 percent involvement may seem self-explanatory, it is really the heart of the matter. Most approaches that brag about 100 percent involvement in making improvements really mean that management (the minority) has decided what problems or work processes employees (the majority) are going to work on and how they are going to go about it. In some cases, especially early in the quality movement, management limited the number of employees involved in these efforts in the mistaken belief that quality improvements required a sophistication that only a few people in the company possessed. But what if you could have employees look at their own jobs critically, looking for ways to improve, finding solutions, and initiating action? That is the kind of involvement that CQP makes possible. Everybody knows their own job better than anyone else in the building. Given a framework and a tool kit, everyone can seize the initiative. Notice the caveat: A tool kit. Not one tool. If, after all, the only tool a homeowner possessed were a hammer, all problems would be treated the same—as nails. But, in virtually all walks of life, problems or challenges are not consistent, in either their nature or their level of complexity. A full tool kit is needed for both repairs and improvements.

Beginning a CQP is a high-energy undertaking for an organization as individuals and teams come to realize, "Management trusts us! And they are going to say 'thank you'!" Employees get caught up in the fun of it all, but CQP needs a stronger validation: Quality is profitable. All of the time, effort, and money spent to get CQP under way is an investment—an investment that promises a healthy return.

Maybe Some Other Time . . .

The very simplicity of the CQP approach is a rationale for senior managers to gloss over its possibilities. A senior manager can look at the various CQP components and say to herself or himself, "Well, that's obvious. Besides, we do that stuff already and we'll get results eventually. We can do this anytime." One such argument surfaced at a workshop for a call center whose annual turnover rate was 300 percent. The CEO was listening to a presentation on CQP when he said, "Why, that's nothing but leadership and a bunch of training," and cut the meeting short. He felt the proposed solution sounded "too easy" to possibly be the answer.

Though it is true that the components named contain no surprises (and that it can be argued that CQP is, essentially, formalized common sense), it is not true that the average company is actively pursuing all of the components at any one time, particularly in a coordinated manner with continual improvement as the unifying objective. The wrinkle, the "new thing" that CQP proposes, is doing everything simultaneously. No one is applauded for juggling just one ball, nor would anyone hire a one-ball juggler to ensure the success of their child's birthday party. It's all or nothing. And the order in which the components are listed has no significance. Communications, for instance, is not the least important component, although it is listed last. It is, rather, one of seven vital concepts that must be brought to life as part of a CQP effort.

That's why senior managers with more imagination look at the components of CQP and immediately assign it to the "too hard" pile. Pursuing seven concepts simultaneously is daunting. Just for starters, senior managers have to invest considerable time, effort, ego, and resources—all in addition to their "normal" jobs—in order to approach what is required by top management commitment and leadership. Hard? You bet. Worse yet, this approach involves sharing power.

Alibis abound for not making the effort. The motivational poster declaration (under the picture of a regal-looking bald eagle) that "If you pursue two rabbits at once, both will escape" is one such argument. Humans, however, are more multifaceted—particularly since their prey can't hop off to the side at the last moment. The insistence by many quality approaches that only one activity can be pursued at a time (much like the too-frequent assertion that all problem-solving steps must be followed in strict sequence for every problem of any size) is counterintuitive. In their personal lives, managers and nonmanagers function comfortably in multitask mode. If the ability to do more than one thing at a time were taken away from the human race, life would grind to a halt.

There are, of course, other reasons or excuses not to pursue continual improvement (one of the code phrases for quality). One is the presentation of quality, in both the popular press and the professional press. Neither has done an adequate job of explaining what quality is and how best to go about achieving it. (This is a case where shooting a few messengers may be justifiable.) With so many conflicting approaches, it's "safer" (executives can argue) to wait until the final answers are in. And shrewd senior managers have probably noticed that, so far as the information put forward by the quality-specific press, there appears to be a correlation between the topics of featured articles and the curricula of professional courses and services offered by the publishing organization. The emphasis on ISO and Six Sigma falls neatly into this category.

Thanks to thinking along those lines, many quality processes were begun mostly for show with no real attempt at a defendable justification—which made them easy to abandon. A primary reason for "doing" quality in those organizations appears to have been a desire to be able to say "yes" when a customer—either an individual consumer or another organization—asked, "Do you have a quality process?" It was also considered a plus if a corporation could make the statement in their annual report or other publications that they were following the latest quality improvement methodology. The number of companies that declared themselves Six Sigma practitioners grew exponentially during the well-publicized last years of Jack Welch's tenure at GE.

Further complicating matters is the fact that this is a lifetime (or at least long-term) endeavor. It's unrealistic to think, "We'll push this quality process until we get everyone in the habit of doing things right. At that point, we can drop the formal stuff because our folks will know what to do." That's akin to saying, "We'll go to church for a couple of years, and once we've heard all the readings once, we can quit going because we'll know how to act." Even when people know something is the right and best thing to do, they still need encouragement, examples, and rewards to maintain a desired behavior.

There is another warning that senior management should keep in mind: Poor judgment at the top can trump improvement at the bottom. As in days of old, if the decision-makers do not correctly point the ship in the right direction, no amount of improvement in rowing techniques is going to get the crew home. Motorola, in the wake of its 1988 Baldrige win, was in the driver's seat in its industry. The company was good and quite provably getting better every day until top management decided to roll the dice on a satellite-dependent communications system. This proved to be a poor move and drained company resources and energy, giving competitors time and opportunity to close the gap.

There is no denying that initiating changes in the name of quality is best suited for a company in the black, a good company that wants to be great. Companies in financial trouble have so many issues at play that adding a quality process (particularly one defined and imposed by a consultant or a consultant working only with senior management) may not help much. Obvious issues need to be addressed before the word *quality* is introduced. If a company is in trouble because of a truly bloated payroll, staff reductions come first or employees will unfairly assume that quality is the cause of their friends being fired or their salary reduced. Once the ship has been steadied a bit—and everybody's attention has been gotten—then quality can be carefully introduced as a way to ensure that the company never gets into that sort of trouble again.

Another caveat: If the situation is such that an organization can either begin a quality effort at a particular point in time or most likely never have another opportunity, then proceeding is the preferred option, regardless of the financial health of the company.

With so many things to consider, it's no wonder that the first priority in CQP is top management commitment.

Simple, but Difficult

Winning commitment begins with understanding the basic nature of a quality process. A person needs to consider two pairs of antonyms: simple versus complex and easy versus difficult. Most human endeavors can be described by combining a word from one of these pairs with a word from the other pair.

Nuclear science, for instance, falls easily into the category of complex (rather than simple) and difficult (rather than easy). It is a complex concept and doing it successfully is a difficult task. Common mythology (as promulgated in popular music and romance novels) has it that falling in love is complex and easy; complex to understand, easy to do.

Quality is made up of simple concepts: "Let's make or do things better than we used to." "We want to be the preferred choice among potential buyers." "We want employees' ideas." "Let's take accurate measurements." Actually defining and implementing a quality process—and carrying through with the relentless, day-to-day work necessary to maintain a continual improvement effort—is not easy. Quality is simple and difficult.

Most quality consultants make their livings convincing senior management groups that achieving quality is just the opposite: complex (and they—the consultants—have arcane knowledge) and easy (if you just let them—the consultants—handle the details). When you've got it that backward, progress is expensive and slow. Senior managers can make most of the decisions about quality by themselves (relatively simple), but seeing it through (relatively difficult) is not for the faint-hearted. Senior managers who put CQP in the "too hard" category are almost right. So why would anyone attempt it?

2 The Economic Case for Quality

FedEx, a Malcolm Baldrige National Quality Award (MBNQA) winner in 1990, operates under the banner "People, Service, Profit." Ritz Carlton, a 1999 winner, stated it best: "Profit is the residue of quality." Both slogans highlight the basic premise of the quality revolution from its very inception: Quality makes money. And though money that comes through the door with customers is the traditional way to measure profit, quality also focuses on unexpended funds that gravitate to the bottom line as a result of improved practices. This argument was at the heart of Phil Crosby's seminal work *Quality Is Free* (1979). Crosby's emphasis on prevention highlighted the reality that it is cheaper to do a job right the first time than to recover from an error. Whether it is reducing employee turnover, streamlining processes, or market testing, every quality initiative gains its legitimacy by linking its use to increased profits.

Where profits fail to rise, quality (and its associated practices) is dismissed as a failure. The *Wall Street Journal*, for instance, took a stand starting in the late 1980s that the pursuit of quality wasn't a topic worthy of their benediction, more than ever after the bankruptcy of Houston-based Wallace Company, a 1990 Baldrige winner. Harping on the company's failure and paying lavish attention to companies whose financial results were mediocre, *WSJ* writers and editors ignored dozens of companies whose fortunes (and stock) rose steadily before and after winning the award. Overall, winners of the MBNQA routinely outpace the Wall Street norms for growth in value by four to one.

The truth is this: Even corporations whose profits have fluctuated after winning the Baldrige affirm that subscribing to the practices embodied in quality gives them the best chance to regain their vitality when the business climate is more favorable to them. John Wallace, owner of the family-owned Wallace Company, ascribed its bankruptcy to a bank failure and management misjudgments. Michael Spies, the CEO, was credited as saying that without quality practices, Wallace Company wouldn't have been around ". . . to enjoy the '91 recession." Quality practices bring profit to the bottom line through customer satisfaction, customer retention, lower overhead, and greater capacity for work. Quality alone, however, does not guarantee success. There is no escaping the fact that businesses operate in a larger environment of governmental policies, international politics, and customer fortunes and misfortunes, and that the business climate today is impacted by forces unimaginable even 50 years ago.

Consumer Power

Consumer power has always been the bedrock of commerce. You cannot provide something people won't buy and survive. This is especially clear when customers have options, which is not always the case.

Think of all the people in the world as being divided into three categories: owners/managers, workers, and consumers. Despite the fact that most people simultaneously fill at least two of these categories at some point in their lives, the groups are virtually always talked about as if they are three separate entities. Pronouncements are made about a particular political/economic decision (e.g., NAFTA) being "good for the consumers" (ignoring or downplaying its effect on owners/managers in lowering profits and/or on workers in delayed pay raises or layoffs) or "good for the workers" (e.g., a new labor pact with large raises that has a negative impact on owners/managers and consumers). Considering them individually illuminates market forces, despite the overlaps between the three groups.

Commercial relationships between these groups change over time. When markets are local and consumers have few options, owners/managers have disproportionate control. They decide what to offer in the marketplace; they choose who will work for them and who will not; and they dictate the wages they pay. They also decide how much they will charge for their product or service. Workers or customers might object, but they have no realistic alternatives. For thousands of years, geographic monopolies in commerce were a reality. It was too expensive for workers or customers to move to another area, even if cultural and legal norms hadn't made it difficult, and options for foreign goods were few. Distant competitors found that shipping costs wiped out any expected advantage in all but luxury goods and shoddy merchandise; communication was too difficult for service options to exist.

This world of casual—and virtually unavoidable—monopolies was challenged in the late nineteenth century following the lowering of financial, legal, and cultural barriers to the movement of people across state lines or across national boundaries. Workers then made a play for some power. That effort evidenced itself in everything from trade unions to socialism to Communism. Even in countries that remained basically capitalistic, workers unions wrested a degree of power from the owners/managers, usually in the form of higher wages and job security.

These gains, however, rarely impinged on the owners'/managers' ability to decide "what" and "how much" and "at what price" for goods and services. Consumers were still virtually powerless. Henry Ford's famous dictum that a customer could have a Model T Ford in any color—as long as it was black—was indicative of this power structure. Markets were still local, for the most part, and customers took what they could get. There were, to be sure, a variety of cheap imported everyday items for consumers, such as textiles, pottery, and footwear, and there were expensive rarities such as Swiss watches, German binoculars, and English bone china in luxury goods. But times were changing. The Sears Roebuck Catalogue provided everything from prefab housing to tea dresses designed by a Paris designer as communication and transportation improved.

The second half of the twentieth century saw an expansion of this phenomenon. When the first boatload of Toyotas reached the California shore in the 1970s, it heralded an age in which the cost to ship completed material to the United States had dropped sufficiently to allow a bulky, expensive item to be made elsewhere, shipped across a good-sized ocean, and offered at a competitive price. In the years that followed, American consumers were amazed to find that foreign-made products—beginning with cars and electronics—often cost less and worked better than what they were used to. Japanese-made copiers, for example, were available for less money than it took the behemoth Xerox to manufacture its copiers in the United States. As part of the scramble to secure market share, "quality control" began to make inroads in manufacturing. Slowly, goods and services were also held to new standards of quality. After the Internet made it possible for consumers to find both products and services across physical distances at a reduced cost, customers, by and large, gained controlling power in the marketplace. Their power to determine "what" and "how much" and "at what price" became explicit, as did the inescapability of global markets.

There are, to be sure, unpleasant side effects to these changes. Unsophisticated consumers have virtually driven American television manufacturers out of the marketplace, wrongly assuming that the high quality they were used to would be delivered at a greatly reduced price. Jobs, including service jobs, became vulnerable to outsourcing as owners/managers shopped for cheap labor. Sometimes this resulted in lower quality; sometimes it didn't. Higher wages and increased buying power in one part of the globe were offset by lower wages and decreased buying power in another. National corporate identities got traded in for global corporate identities.

The challenge for every nation is to retain control of its prosperity by bringing capital from the rest of the world into its banking system. A nation's goods and services have to be able to compete in the global, and increasingly incestuous, marketplace. Being seen as a quality alternative in a sufficient number of market niches is key. Over time, in a free market, quality commands a higher price (people will pay up front to avoid future problems) and it is cheaper to produce (less waste in activities and materials). Establishing eternal subsidies to enable a country's companies to compete based on price is a case of robbing Peter to pay Paul. National leaders can do far more long-term good by finding ways to encourage continual improvement than by interfering with the operations of a free market.

In sum, what is important is that after much mucking about by thousands of companies, the basic truth holds: Capturing and keeping customers is the bedrock of profit. And even if business leaders may have grown weary of the word *quality*, customers haven't. *Quality* remains an oft-repeated claim in print ads and on TV and radio because advertisers know that customers respond to the word. Consumers, both corporate and individual, prefer to buy stuff that does, at the least, what they expect it to do. They tell their friends when things meet their expectations and when they don't. And they remain loyal when their expectations have been satisfied. When customers have options, they reward quality and punish laggard organizations, both in the marketplace and in the stock market. Quality, and the expectation of quality, is a vital force in the marketplace for customer satisfaction and retention.

Capacity for Work

Capacity for work is an important concept at the heart of understanding the economic value of quality. Beginning a quality effort implicitly asks the question, "Let's see if we can improve our procedures so that we can do this job with fewer resources." This is conceptually sound, but it can lead to serious problems when members of an organization read "people" for "resources." This immediately puts a serious damper on their creativity: No one thinks getting themselves or a friend fired is a particularly good idea. Needless to say, this approach to improvement does not go over well with workers, whether organized or unorganized. Automakers and their unions have been in a state of warfare for decades in large part because of the manufacturers' attempts at decreasing the number of people on the payroll.

In other words, one option for appearing to be more successful is firing some people and keeping the pressure on the remaining employees to produce the same numbers that were being cranked out pre-downsizing. To do so means, by maintaining the same overall value, that the survivors are being "more productive." Reengineering headed down this path with the result that organizations redesigned themselves to handle their current customer base perfectly—while creating serious morale problems and being unprepared for the future.

A more positive approach is, "Let's see if we can improve our procedures so that we can accomplish more with the people we have." This effort may include simply taking fuller advantage of the talents already on the payroll. Depending on the culture of the company and the track record of management/employee relationships, it may be necessary to make a specific promise along the lines of, "No one will be separated from the payroll because of the implementation of quality. If an idea eliminates your current job, you will be offered another at the same or higher pay rate." When such a promise is believed, the objective becomes believable, employees become more cooperative, and organizations redesign themselves to increase capacity.

This is the difference between productivity and quality. The failure to understand and/or explain this difference has often made winning the support of unions—which have too frequently suffered job losses in the wake of productivity programs—challenging. A simple division problem can illustrate the difference to the skeptical.

Consider two components: resources as the denominator and outputs as the numerator. Both can be measured and combined to assess how well an enterprise is doing. In both productivity and quality, the objective is to increase the number of outputs per resource. It doesn't matter what the outputs are (cars, newspapers, apples, loans, customers served, etc.) or what the resources are (people, money, raw materials, etc.)—the goal is to increase the value of the fraction formed by dividing outputs by resources.

Harking back to grade-school math, there are two ways to increase the value of a fraction. You can decrease the denominator (the resources) or you can increase the numerator (the outputs). If, for instance, you started with the fraction 60/4, the value would be 15. Changing the denominator to a smaller number—making it a 3 instead of a 4— would increase the value to 20. Leaving the denominator at 4 but increasing the numerator to 80 would also yield a value of 20. Generally speaking, doing the first is what passes for productivity; doing the second is what has come to be called *quality*. Announcing what *should* happen, however, won't get the job done. Employees must have tools, training, and trust before they can eliminate wasted motion. That's where CQP comes in.

Show Me the Money

The stumbling block in working on the numerator is that it takes time to see results in the bottom line. More than one quality effort has floundered on this issue. Numerator or denominator, whatever the approach, the simple fact is that it is often difficult to draw a straight line between money claimed as hard dollar savings by employing quality practices and the bottom line. And it is even harder to connect the dots between soft dollar savings (time saved, valued at so-much per hour) and profit. Even when quality is successfully deployed, analysis of savings takes systematic effort. But it can be done—and done honestly—using the concept of capacity for work.

Picture a department with an annual budget of $100,000 for "things" that will help it work more productively. Before being told exactly what their budget for things is to be in a given year, the leadership team of the department would most likely have made up a prioritized list of things that they envisioned, if purchased, would help make the department better at its job. If that list had 10 items on it and the $100,000 only bought the first six of them, the department would essentially be barred from maximizing its results.

Imagine now that item 7 had a cost of $8500 and, thanks to one or more employee ideas, the department recorded a savings of $9000 in hard dollars. That is, $9000 that it had in its budget for, perhaps, buying paper is now available. This could be because of a reduction in expected paper purchases resulting from an idea that consisted solely of asking people, "Do you really need that report every day? With all those pages?" and then not printing the unneeded reports and/or pages.

It would be the very rare department head who would send the $9000 back to the comptroller for distribution among the shareholders. For one thing, the comptroller (once he or she recovered from the shock of having funds returned) would probably transfer the $9000 to some other department that would happily spend it.

In the real world, virtually all departments would use the saved money to buy item 7, quietly setting $500 aside to go toward item #8. Is there a direct line between the saved-by-a-quality-idea $9000 and the bottom line? Not immediately—but the department's ability to produce the product or service it is supposed to produce has been enhanced by the measurable improvement introduced by the newly purchased item 7.

It is possible, for instance, that with item 7 integrated into the workflow, the department can produce 310 units per week rather than the previous 300. That means that over a year, it can produce 520 more units (10 units × 52 weeks) than it could have before the idea was implemented and the budget savings were realized and reinvested. The capacity for work has been increased with no increase in personnel and without going outside of the budget.

What about the soft dollars, the savings in time that are so frequently the result of an employee idea? If, for instance, an idea is put in place that saves 11 minutes in a daily procedure, it doesn't usually grab a lot of attention. But what if that time-saving change applies to 90 people? That's a savings of 990 minutes—16.5 hours—every day . . . or 82.5 hours a week . . . or 4290 hours a year. When expressed in dollars, the company just avoided hiring two people (given an average work year in America of 2080 hours—minus vacation time, sick time, personal days, etc.). The collective capacity for work of the 90 people already on the job has been effectively increased to a point that previously would have required 92. It is as if the company had managed to find two people who would work for free and who were already experienced at whatever task the original 90 folks are doing.

Does that increase in capacity for work show up on the bottom line? Total hours saved can be tracked, of course, and given a value to give an indication of the impact of the ideas, but the answer is more ambiguous. If the workflow is static, then excess capacity has been created and no profits accrue. For instance, if the department previously was receiving and handling 270 units (3 per person) of work per day (or 70,200 per year), it can accurately be argued that saving 11 minutes per person per day made it possible for the department to increase its capacity for work and handle 1560 more units of work ([the 6 additional units for the 2 virtual people] × [5 days a week] × [52 weeks]) at no increase in cost. The 90 people who used to take care of the production of 70,200 units per year now handle 71,760. This is only academically interesting if the incoming workload is the same. But if the workload increased by 6 units per day, the size of the department could remain unchanged at 90. It is possible (and reasonable) to generalize about the impact of a series of time-saving ideas on a workplace and test those assumptions in an organization.

A more specific example: In 2000, the associates of the UICI Insurance Center Agent Licensing Department immediately grasped the opportunity that CQP gave them to control their own work procedures. At the time, there were 14 associates in the Licensing Department—a slightly oversized Quality Team that, year-in and year-out, was one of the most active in the company.

In 1999, the Licensing Department handled 100 "hirepacks" for new agents (insurance salesmen and saleswomen) per week; in 2004, they handled between 350 and 374 per week. In 1999, they did the licensing and paperwork for the appointment of 3970 new agents; in 2003, the number was 9989. Number of associates in the department in 2004: 14. Essentially, they greatly increased the numerator while holding the denominator steady.

On the other hand, if a series of ideas that claimed substantial time savings were implemented without a change in the output-per-resource ratio, it would be reasonable to question the validity of the savings claimed. Before jumping to conclusions, it might be worth investigating whether the current output is measurably better than the previous output, implicitly because the workers finally have enough time to do things correctly. In that case, the savings/impact could be expected to show up in fewer returns and happier customers. But such analysis takes time and effort, and when the results are incremental—when a person or a team has an idea for improvement that "only" saves a little time or a few dollars—many organizations mistakenly conclude that neither the improvement nor the analysis is worth the effort.

A Case Study of Profit

At the UICI Insurance Center, a CQP was implemented in September 2000. Three years later, due to a quantum leap in the sales abilities and results of its two field agencies, the dollar amount of the new policies being submitted increased to a level 350 percent of what it was in 1999. The number of employees in the company increased from approximately 800 to about 1150, or approximately 45 percent. How is that possible?

Part of the answer is in increased capacity for work. During those years, the CQP recorded more than $12.8 million in soft dollar savings and more than $9.2 million in hard dollar savings. Saved time was valued at $15 per hour. Dividing the $12.8 million by $15 yields 853,333, and dividing that by 2000 (average number of hours in an employee work year) results in a figure of 427—accounting for 427 employees who were not hired. The remaining difference can safely be credited to hard dollar savings that were used to buy equipment that would otherwise not have been affordable.

In both the time saved and the money saved, the impact was on the company's capacity for work. Previously, employees could handle only x amount of work (and then only with a great deal of overtime). After three years of a CQP effort, they could handle $3.5x$, even though there were fewer than $0.5x$ more people and overtime had been cut dramatically. The company's capacity for work had outstripped increases in the number of employees on its payroll and the pace of the growth in its budget. In short, the company increased the numerator by a great deal while increasing the denominator by a relatively small amount.

Serendipitously, shortly after the first anniversary of their CQP effort in late 2001, top managers at the Insurance Center were given an opportunity to compare several parameters of their process to a Six Sigma effort at another insurance company. A nine-page article in *Best's Review*, an insurance industry magazine, examined the activities and goals at Conseco Insurance Company, evaluating progress in the eighth month of the effort. Conseco had decided on a Six Sigma approach after hiring GE veteran Gary C. Wendt, a disciple of Jack Welch and one of the executives who had been considered as his replacement. The Six Sigma goal was $100,000,000 in annualized savings in the first year. With 14,000 employees, that averaged out to approximately $7150 in savings per employee. Offsetting the savings was an enormous expense: 170 Six Sigma professionals (plus the department head and her staff) were described as being "dedicated exclusively" to the effort.

The Insurance Center began with the goal of involving every employee in identifying savings and with no specific dollar figure in mind; they established a Quality Department of two analysts, a department head, and no outside consultants. At the end of the first year, the company of 800 employees had realized a savings of $5,414,985, or approximately $6770 per employee. When the article about Conseco was written with four months to go until the year was up, 3 percent of their projects ($214.50 per employee) had been completed. Attempts to contact Conseco to track further progress were rebuffed.

Conseco's experience was another example of top management misjudgment trumping an effort to improve quality. Wendt had been hired in June 2000 to reverse falling stock prices after management had OK'd the $6 billion acquisition of Green Tree Financial and a $95 million sponsorship deal with the Indiana Pacers that included naming rights for Conseco Fieldhouse. Despite a huge investment in Six Sigma, the company declared bankruptcy in December 2002, reemerging in September 2004. Wendt resigned in October of that same year.

At the Insurance Center, an additional contribution to the bottom line was made by a lower turnover rate. Turnover can serve as both a best measure of corporate health and an accurate predictor of future performance. Low turnover indicates a workforce that chooses to be there and whose morale is high, as well as promising that the average level of experience in the organization is rising steadily.

The Bureau of Labor Statistics national data show that the average turnover rate in 2003, regardless of industry, was 38 percent. In the financial services industry it was 22 percent. Here are the figures for UICI:

1998	50.0%
1999	28.0%
2000	30.0% (CQP effort began in September 2000)
2001	20.0%
2002	17.1%
2003	15.6%
2004	11.7%

The same leadership capabilities that were needed for the initiation and maintenance of a CQP were also engaged in a number of morale-building initiatives during that period, but the inclusiveness of employees in decision making through CQP was a major contributor to the stability of the organization.

Top Management Commitment

Profit, then, is the compelling motivation for beginning a quality process. And profit is an argument that employees understand. Top managers have the obligation to explain the importance of quality in ways that employees find compelling, and the arguments that swayed the executives in the first place are often the best:

1. **Quality makes money.** It increases an organization's capacity for work, it saves resources (a key point for governmental and non-profit organizations), and it helps to make the organization's products and services more competitive. As pointed out earlier in the chapter, well-made products cost less to produce (due in large part to not having a waste expense figured into its cost to produce) and command higher prices.

2. **Quality leads to loyal customers.** Customers who are "delighted" or "satisfied" are so because they have a pleasant memory about their most recent specific experience. Loyal customers are more valuable because they come back. And they bring their friends. They even forgive an organization—up to a point—and they can often be convinced to coproduce with the company, meaning they will take the time to help design new products and services by filling out forms, accepting invitations to join focus groups, and being "samplers." Or by registering complaints before they become real problems.

3. **Quality leads to loyal employees.** Employees who are loyal stick around, they bring their prescreened friends down to the company to hire on, they forgive an organization—up to a point—and they build an environment in which other employees thrive, an environment in which everyone has an opportunity to contribute.

4. **Quality is the ethical thing to do.** If making money (or saving resources) isn't a motivator, if the benefits that come from having loyal customers and/or loyal employees aren't motivators, then settle for this legal and moral benefit: It's ethical. What a quality process really does is make it possible for an organization to deliver on its promises, implicit and explicit. Including promises it has made to itself.

These are four primary reasons why the pursuit of excellence (another code phrase for quality) is well worth the investment in time, resources, and cash. Perhaps to avoid sounding too capitalistic, quality process advocates put forward all manner of reasons to pursue quality—including environmental concerns, human dignity issues, and national competitiveness . . . all of which are valid. But the bottom line remains the bottom line.

Quality . . . performance excellence . . . continual improvement . . . whatever . . . the point has always been, "Is your organization functioning better today than it was yesterday?" and "Can you reasonably expect that it will be measurably better tomorrow?" If top managers want the answer to these questions to be a resounding "Yes," then the next step is to translate conviction into action.

3 | Active Commitment at the Top

D efining, implementing, and maintaining a solid quality process with positive short- and long-term impact is not easy. Remember: simple but difficult. The individuals who sit in the executive offices must be prepared for the challenges and expense necessary to create an environment in which subordinates can implement improvements. In addition to investing individual time and ego, commitment means a willingness to spend money on a structure to support employee involvement. Ultimately, a Complete Quality Process is notably less expensive than Six Sigma, ISO, reengineering, and various other efforts of the past. But it does require a capital outlay up front.

Getting started depends on doing first things first. And second things first. And third things first. A CQP entails many activities happening virtually simultaneously to capture momentum. There must be a solid blueprint for action, as well as somebody to read that blueprint and make sure it is followed or, when not followed precisely, intentionally modified and then followed. Identifying who will be responsible for creating the blueprint, who will check it for applicability to the organization, and who will be responsible for its day-to-day operation puts a face on quality.

Putting a Face on Quality

A great many quality efforts in the United States and elsewhere during the last two decades of the twentieth century could most honestly be labeled "quality by proclamation." This is what happens when the head of an organization declares publicly that his or her organization is going to be a "quality organization" or "the quality standard-bearer for the industry" without having a specific, effective plan in mind for making that happen. The declaration is usually followed by a series of awareness efforts in the form of speeches, articles in company publications, and the ever-popular posters hanging on hallway and cafeteria walls.

Regardless of how charismatic the high-ranking official of the organization is (or thinks he or she is), no matter how well articulated the goal is, it's not going to work. Quality with a face but no substance is disingenuous. The organization is changing its rules. Employees need to know what the new rules are or, except for the bravest of souls, they are not going to take the chance of acting on what they think the new rules might (or should) be. An explicit set of instructions lets everyone know exactly how they can take part in the continual improvement effort.

With this warning in mind, where does management begin? When the senior leadership team gives its informed consent to the idea of a CQP, there will be an initial flurry of activity, much of which won't be evident to most folks in the company. The first truly visible indication that the organization is serious about quality comes when it is time to decide who will be the guide. This individual's responsibilities will include both pointing executives and employees toward appropriate long-term goals and leading them through short-term challenges. He or she must be in sync with whatever methodology the company settles on.

If the preferred methodology is one that takes advantage of the skills, knowledge, and interests of every person on the payroll (in short, a CQP), finding someone to head up the effort is automatically more interesting than it would be if a more conventional approach were chosen. Picking someone to head up a conventional effort is relatively simple: The search committee finds someone with the appropriate certification, checks for a personality match, and they are pretty much finished. The certificates, belts, credentials, and conventional wisdom that come with a traditional quality guy (*guy* being a genderless word in this context) may, however, constitute too much baggage in a CQP. If, for instance, during an early interview, the prospective head of quality says anything akin to, "This will take a long time and cost a lot of money," the search committee should thank the candidate for his or her time and move on.

Finding someone to lead a CQP effort requires what is commonly referred to as thinking outside the box. (More accurately, not just outside the box, but far enough away from the box that it can't even be seen clearly.) So what characteristics should the company leadership be looking for? For starters, a blend of common sense, business sense, and a basic knowledge of quality will do nicely. The first two have to be evident at the time of hiring; knowledge of quality can expand after being hired. Awareness of the various tools that have been introduced in the name of quality is a plus only so far as the person recognizes their status as tools of roughly equal value. Anyone who is reluctant to admit that each tool is appropriate only for particular challenges, while wildly inappropriate for others, is unlikely to have the flexibility needed for CQP.

Experience in the quality world is not necessarily good or bad. Willingness to learn is a more important trait and may be the saving grace of someone who was previously committed to a more conventional quality discipline. Add to the list of qualifications a comfortable relationship with math, a sense of humor, and the ability to communicate, and a company has the basic traits of a competent quality honcho (or quality honcha; again, gender is not a consideration). The ability to communicate may be the most important trait of all. Communication skills (which are, of course, an important part of leadership) take the form of written and verbal, one-on-one, one-on-many, and many-on-one. What is "many-on-one"? The willingness and ability to listen to the employee population's direct and indirect efforts to communicate upward.

Because extensive expert status is not a requirement, candidates need not be from outside the organization. A well-respected operational person in the middle-manager or higher ranks would bring the advantage of already knowing the company. Learning the idiosyncrasies of the people who make up the company and how they work together on a personal and professional basis is more difficult than learning how to plot quality improvements on a chart.

One caution: Overseeing the quality process cannot be seen as a way to beef up the résumé of someone competing for future power in the company. Make no mistake, the position described is second only to president or CEO in terms of personal satisfaction. (For most people, nothing beats being the boss.) This individual is in the middle of virtually everything that is going on in the organization; he or she has the opportunity not only to deal with people throughout the company, but also to see them at their best and happiest. The activities of the quality process are enormously interesting and have a measurable positive impact on the bottom line. But the success of the quality effort cannot be seen as a stepping stone for one individual, or the cooperation of other senior executives will be understandably curtailed.

Broadening the visibility of top management commitment comes in the form of a committee with a blend of people who are seen as having power, translated as the ability to implement decisions without passing them up the line for further approval. This committee is responsible for working out the components of the quality process with the help of whoever is tapped to run the process. For that reason, committee members must be able to articulate the concerns and ideas of employees at all levels. Even if, in reality, the majority of the final decisions reached by the committee are very much an endorsement of an approach created by the quality honcho/honcha, the backing of this group is essential. The company's approach to quality can't be seen as "his program" or "her program"; it must truly be the company's program.

Obviously, decisions need to be made in a timely manner, which becomes more likely when the facilitator of this committee is the individual responsible for the day-to-day operations of the quality effort. The risk is that this individual may attempt to impose a set of definitions and standards that he or she is comfortable with. If the committee is seen as (or perceives itself to be) little more than a rubber stamp for the honcho's/honcha's preconceived notions, the word will get out and interest will wane. There is a balancing act involved. The individual's task is to listen carefully for insights into the culture of the organization and its recent history, while actively engaging in the design process. On one hand is the hazard of appearing to be too directive; on the other, if the honcho/honcha fails to contribute sufficiently, it raises questions about why he/she was hired in the first place.

Educating members of the committee using a series of discussion points makes it possible for them to explain decisions to others in the company, both formally and informally. Agenda items can include questions as fundamental as, "What is quality?" and "What constitutes a quality idea—versus someone doing his (or her) job?" Another agenda item might be a discussion of the implications of the statement, "Responsibility is the obligation to act, authority is the power to act, and accountability is measuring and reporting the act." Committee members can look at the best way to create a structure and vocabulary to provide for all three. To aid the evolution of the committee's thinking, one option is to invite speakers from organizations with solid track records in the area of quality/continual improvement. A quick look at the lists of Baldrige winners and state quality award winners suggests possible guests; another option is to play the videotapes/DVDs of the winners, produced by the NIST (National Institute of Standards and Technology) each year.

The company cannot, however, afford for the committee to become a friendly debating society whose gentle conversations stretch out over months and even years—as has happened with astounding regularity around the country. One of the facilitator's responsibilities is to bring a sense of urgency to the meetings, and one way to do this is to report on progress on decisions made at previous meetings. Overall, the committee will be most productive if it meets weekly until shortly after the process is launched. A high level of attendance is required. Employees, who quite often know exactly where their bosses are, need to see that quality is able to command the time of a group of important people—every week.

A Case Study in Top Management Commitment

At the UICI Insurance Center, the decision to pursue quality was made toward the end of 1999. It was driven by senior managers at the corporate level and supported by the then-current head of the Insurance Center, a subsidiary of UICI. No particular preconceptions were dictated to the headhunter who was hired to find someone who could help establish a quality process.

Among the individuals the corporate recruiter contacted was a coauthor of this book, Pat Townsend. After a dozen years on the speakers circuit, the challenge of returning to the corporate world held some serious attraction—if for no other reason than to see if all of the things he and his coauthor had been telling audiences for over a decade could in fact be done in the twenty-first century.

A couple of interviews later, an offer was made and accepted. Among the reasons for the quick acceptance were the facts that (a) the company had only made one previous ineffectual attempt at quality; there would be minimal cleanup to do, (b) it was evident that the people in the company liked each other; the organization was not at war with itself, and (c) senior management appeared to understand that, even though the company was in the black, the primary reason to make the investment in quality was to make money. Management also appreciated that a quality effort, if well done, would make their customers and their employees happy, and that the pursuit of quality was the ethical thing to do, but for UICI executives, the bottom line was the bottom line.

Looking at the hire from the standpoint of UICI, the candidate had an unusual résumé: 20 years in the Marine Corps, four years as director of a quality process at Paul Revere Insurance Group, two years directing quality at a computer company, over 10 years as a speaker/consultant, and six books and several hundred articles on quality and related topics. Though a military background may seem an incongruous asset in the field of quality, the skills acquired as a Marine were, indeed, invaluable.

Military veterans tend to fall into one of two categories: the minority who believe and act out the stiff, unbending stereotype and the majority who actually paid attention in leadership classes. If the candidate falls into the stereotypical role (which will be easy to spot), he or she will not succeed as the head of a wide-ranging effort that varies every day, such as a CQP effort. If not, the military teaches leadership and communication skills, requires flexibility, and tends to encourage common sense.

One of the early decisions made about the quality process at the Insurance Center was what to call the new hire. Titles have importance, both internally and externally, even if they are rarely used internally. Folks aspire to certain titles, and there is a whole set of assumptions attached to words that show up on business cards. In this case, the title chosen was new to the company: chief quality officer (CQO). "Chief" was chosen specifically to signal to the vice presidents that the person in charge of quality was not competing for the job of president, because it is generally accepted to mean, "at the top of his or her chosen field in this company," where he or she is usually assumed to be content. (Granted, the occasional chief financial officer makes the move to president or CEO, but the moves are unusual enough to merit news coverage.) It was reasoned that "chief" was sufficiently neutral to remove at least one obstacle to future cooperation from other executives. On the other hand, the title "chief quality officer" gave the position sufficient prestige in the eyes of the folks below senior management and people from other companies,.

A powerful boost to the quality effort was supplied shortly after the CQO's arrival. A gentleman with a vague title in the Actuarial Department told him, "I want you to know that I saw a program like this fail at my last company, but I think it has great potential and I am going to promise you right now that I will support this effort." At the time, the CQO welcomed the statement as an encouraging vote of confidence. When this same gentleman, Phil Myhra, was named the new president/CEO of the Insurance Center a month later, his commitment became a foundation stone for the eventual success of the process.

Myhra introduced the mantra, "Mission, Quality, and Culture. Mission is what we do. Quality is how we do it. Culture is how we work together to get it done." As an articulate, concise expression of the direction in which the company was heading, it was deceptively simple—deceptive because it sounded so obvious and so easy. What has come to be known as corporate culture is present in every organization. It is the collection of habits and expectations that define how the people who make up an organization get through the day. The trick is to not let it take shape by chance. It is possible to guide, measure, enforce, and encourage a corporate culture to grow in a specific direction, although the change in culture will ultimately take place at its own pace. Influencing the change can be done by consistently insisting on specific behavior, by providing the training and environment that make the behavior possible, and by setting the example.

A well-implemented quality process can be a major contributor in an effort to customize a company's culture because, as Myhra put it, "Quality is the lubricant that makes it possible for all of the parts of the company to work together." The culture in a company with a well-defined emphasis on quality is different from one where that emphasis is absent; the simple fact that a quality effort begins with a determination to involve every employee destines it to have a major impact on how folks work with each other. But the assumption that a company culture automatically changes to accommodate a quality process is absurd. One of the major responsibilities of the CQO and the Quality Department is to influence corporate culture by making the link between mission and quality. The CQO has an unacknowledged, unofficial position as "chief culture officer" or "chief culture-changing officer."

In recognition of this fact and with the trust and backing of the senior management team, the Quality Department set out their vision statement:

The Vision of the UICI Insurance Center Quality Department

"We will be the catalyst for the continual improvement of the Insurance Center's operational effectiveness and for the realization of the company's cultural values."

The president/CEO and the CQO became active partners in making the mantra a reality. Myhra understood from the outset that he needed to invest his time, intellectual and emotional resources, and energy to make any effort a success; the CQO was able to offer suggestions as to how to best leverage his boss's time and efforts.

Although such mutual support might exist without being quite so explicit, the president/CEO and the CQO in any quality effort are in it together, and efforts to create an environment that encourages continual improvement will fail if either of them falters.

Extending top management commitment throughout the executive suite began shortly after the CQO arrived in early February 2000. The CQO proposed a series of four half-day workshops in March— four consecutive Wednesday mornings—for all managers and above. To set the stage for the workshops, he set out to meet those folks whose commitment and leadership would be critical to the success of the effort. The idea behind the one-on-one meetings was to introduce himself to the leaders of the organization and to allay fears about him being a doctrinaire advocate of one specific way to measure and do everything. Having individual conversations minimized the possibility of executives feeling as if they had been ambushed and trapped into supporting something about which they had no say.

Class participants walked into the first of the four classes with their defenses lowered and with some knowledge of what was going to be suggested, beginning with a commitment to 100 percent employee involvement. They were also aware that their input would be welcome. The four classes were titled Leadership, Participation, Measurement, and How Are We Going To Do This? The first three consisted of guided, but open, discussions about aspects of a CQP; the fourth got down to pragmatic questions of how to go about translating concepts into something useful and doable.

One question raised by a manager during the second class was particularly interesting: "OK, we've agreed to do this. Why not start right now?" The question opened the door to a detailed discussion of why it would be inadvisable. The CQO said that, while he loved the idea of starting immediately, there was a substantial list of reasons why it couldn't be done, beginning with the lack of a Quality Department (except for the CQO) and a tracking system and database. As a compromise, the committee decided to develop a computer-based suggestion program to run until the "real" quality process was put in place. It was theorized that doing so would serve to introduce the word *quality* into the company vocabulary, as well as plant the idea that change was possible and that suggestions would be welcome.

Two days later, the CQO received a call from one of the managers who had attended the class, inviting him to visit the manager's desk. Once there, he was shown an Access database program incorporating every feature he had listed for a computer-based suggestion system. There were two results: One was that the CQO added creative, computer-savvy manager John Fynn to the Quality

Department (doubling its size to two); the other was that the suggestion system was in place shortly after the four half-day classes were completed. The rapid implementation of the computer-based suggestion program helped to establish a needed sense of urgency and encourage employees to talk about quality and anticipate future developments.

At the end of the four workshops, attendees had agreed to proceed in five areas:

1. The beginning of the education/communications effort to make *quality* a natural part of the company vocabulary;

2. The addition of another person to the Quality Department;

3. The formation of a Quality Steering Committee (QSC) as a functioning component of the overall quality effort;

4. The establishment of the actual day-to-day mechanics of the quality process; and

5. The definition and construction of a quality idea tracking program and database.

The fourth class took an interesting turn when, early in the first hour, Phil Myhra, newly appointed as the president/CEO, turned to the rest of the class and said, "Wait. I need to ask a question. Are we prepared to do this? How many want to go ahead with this the way he's laid it out and explained it during these classes? I'd like to see a show of hands." After a brief pause, all of the hands went up. In all honesty, in view of the fact that Myhra obviously thought the five areas laid out for pursuing quality were a good idea, it would have been surprising for anyone to keep both hands on the table; but the fact remains that, no matter how pure the motivation of each of the hand-raisers may have been, all hands were up and a public, mutual pledge to proceed was sealed.

To underscore that the vote was a realistic reflection of the group's acceptance, virtually everybody in the classes volunteered to be on the QSC, making it easy to populate that group. The QSC became responsible for working with the CQO on the details of a 100 percent employee-involvement structure as had been discussed in the classes. Forming the QSC was one way to ensure that the quality effort at the Insurance Center was adapted to fit with the existing culture and support the company's mission. A CQP must be positioned so that it is within reach of current practices and habits, but it must at the same time demand improvements. Once initial steps are taken and the mission, quality, and culture are aligned, the Quality

Department and QSC can push the bar up a bit further. No group, short of a tremendous crisis (and then only for a short time), will jump from A to Z. They will, however, go with careful and informed leadership from A to B. And then from B to C. And on toward Z, step by step.

One important question addressed several times in the course of the four classes was how long it would take to "get from here to there"—that is, from the day when there was an informed decision made by senior management to proceed to the day when a functioning process was in place. The answer from the still-new CQO was always the same: "From six to eight months for an organization of this size—or any organization with fewer than 3000 people." When, after all of the conversation and all of the classes, the show of hands resulted in a unanimous response in March, an informed decision had been made. The clock was running. Six months would be up in late September. (The kick-off date was actually September 14, 2000.)

In 1983, the Quality Steering Committee at the Paul Revere Insurance Group was composed of the senior managers from each of the major departments in the company. In 2000, the Quality Steering Committee at the UICI Insurance Center had not only senior executives, mostly volunteers from the four half-day classes, but also invitees from the ranks of managers and supervisors who had been recommended as being knowledgeable about the company culture. The QSC's size was perhaps bigger than an ideal committee, but its advantage was that there were both senior and junior representatives from every department. Associates in the company, if they had thought to, could have looked at the committee and picked out the two or more people who represented them. As at Paul Revere, the committee continued to evolve in the following years to include additional nonmanagement employees who demonstrated particular enthusiasm and skill for the quality process.

One early activity that occasioned spirited discussion while helping QSC members come to grips with, and then articulate, what they saw as the role of the to-be-defined approach was choosing a name for the process. At the UICI Insurance Center, the choice that won the vote was the phrase "Quality First," accompanied by a logo that could have been taken as either an outline of the company building or a set of building blocks. This was imagery enough for everyone while saying to the company: "Quality is crucial." Although the identities of individuals submitting suggestions were withheld until after the voting, the "Quality First" logo was the creation of John Fynn of the Quality Department. It was a perfect complement to Myhra's "Mission, Quality, and Culture."

Throughout April, May, and June, the QSC and CQO worked on aligning quality and culture at the Insurance Center, agreeing on an approach. The heart of the process would be quality teams implementing quality ideas and using a quality idea tracking program and database to let the Quality Department know what the team had done. Once notification of the implementation of an idea was entered, one of the two quality analysts (the admittedly underdescriptive name initially used for the positions held by Fynn and Candace Whelan, the third member of the Quality Department) would review the idea, verifying all calculations and confirming the impact of the idea. The company would then acknowledge the improvement by saying "thank you." Subsequent chapters will cover the reasons for and implications of these decisions.

In the middle of these activities was the Quality Department, providing stability and knowledge while encouraging change. The identification of the members of the Quality Department initiated the discussion of exactly what the format of the process would be (beginning with a new department member asking, "Now, what is it you want me to do?"). And following up on the suggestion program gave the education/communications effort a solid beginning place. It should be noted that while neither John Fynn nor Candace Whelan had any previous experience in the field of quality, they did have exactly the traits that the CQO was looking for: very bright, very well-respected, wonderfully creative, and possessing more than enough experience in the company to know how the pieces fit together. It is, quite simply, easier for bright, well-respected, creative, knowledgeable people to learn the various quality mechanics than it is to hire a quality specialist off the street and have him or her learn the company and win the trust of managers and supervisors.

Sustaining Commitment at the Top

Increased profits are the main motivation to support quality over the long haul, but they are not the only incentive. Senior managers are often delighted to find that the existence of a quality process facilitates strategic planning. While the mission of the corporation may stay constant ("to make the best darn widgets in the world"), strategic plans are usually updated on an annual basis to give the company a solid statement of what the organization needs to do in the coming year. A quality process interacts with the strategic plan both to determine its content and to assure its implementation. Properly trained, a member of the Quality Department can also serve as a facilitator at meetings to spell out the plan. Having someone with a fresh set of eyes, knowledgeable about the industry in general and the building of strategic plans in particular, can make the process more productive.

Input into the strategic plan comes from the CQP database. This information enables executives to be realistic about what is possible. One of the things that makes the construction of strategic plans more difficult in the twenty-first century is the fact that virtually every segment of a company is now computer-based. This is particularly true with a service, paper-and-ideas company, but it is also true to an increasing degree in organizations of all sorts. Few changes are made that don't require the involvement of the Information Technology (IT) Department. What that means in the real world is that the head of a department can rarely blurt out the commitment, "Yeah, my folks can do that before the end of the year." The true statement is, "If we can get enough time from the IT folks and some new hardware and software, we can install it and be ready to go before the end of the year." The problem is, of course, that the IT Department has only a finite number of resources—both people and budget. A CQP database reflects areas in which IT support was requested in the past year. It also provides a genuine look at what issues employees chose to tackle in the recent past, what resources were available to them, what challenges remain unmet, and how employee-based activities align with previous strategic plans.

At the Insurance Center, the Quality Department is responsible for communicating the results of the strategic plan to all the employees, linking mission, quality, and culture. Once promulgated, the plan is intended to serve as a resource when quality teams ask the question "Are we doing the right things?" and as a guide when a team is trying to decide what to work on next.

Long-term commitment is also sustained by membership on quality teams. When everyone, including vice presidents, managers, and supervisors, is a member of a team, it puts commitment on public display. This avoids the inevitable loss of interest in quality at the management level when the CQO, QSC, and Quality Department are instructed to "go ahead and do quality" while the management team gets back to doing "real work." Phil Myhra's mantra was instrumental in making it clear that quality was not something that management had others do in addition to their normal jobs; quality was how everyone in the organization did their everyday jobs.

Team membership at all levels also deals with the difficulty of defining the phrase *top management*. The words mean different things to different people. The first and most obvious definition is "the president/CEO and his or her direct reports." A wider definition is "anyone perceived as having power." This definition encompasses even the ranks of supervisors. In fact, for most employees, the definition could be most accurately put as, "If you can make my immediate boss sweat, you're top management."

With that definition, anyone who is two hierarchical layers above anyone else in the organization is, for CQP purposes, a top manager. In this case, the minimum necessary level of commitment moves beyond the intellectual commitment of the majority of these managers to active participation. Membership on a quality team, however, will necessitate changes in how leaders think about their organization and the employees on the payroll. For all but the very few, commitment will call for changes in personal leadership style.

4 Leading with Confidence

Complete Quality Process presents a paradox: The first step in implementation is an authoritarian decision that everyone in the organization will focus on quality; the next step consists of participatory decisions on what approach best fits the corporate culture; and the final step involves delegating decision-making power to all employees. Perhaps the best summation of the journey from authoritarian to delegative was offered by Chuck Soule, co-chairman of the Quality Steering Committee at Paul Revere Insurance Group (the committee that designed the first CQP): "Top-down commitment; bottom-up implementation."

Creating the environment that not only allows but also encourages employee participation in improving quality is a major challenge. Jack Welch, legendary leader of GE, has been quoted as saying, "The hard side of quality is the soft side." Many senior executives in a reasonable conversation or on a written test will give the correct answer when asked if delegating is a good idea. But letting subordinates in on decision making is tough, as is asking for help from people who were not previously thought of as fonts of knowledge and ideas. After all, isn't it a basic belief that organizations are meritocracies in which one rises to the top by being smarter and/or working harder than anyone else?

The success of a CQP, however, depends not only on giving every employee a tool kit, but also on inculcating the ability and the will to use the tools. In fact, it can be argued that the ability and will to use the tools are paramount. And that's where leadership comes in. Tom Peters once said that the problem with most quality efforts is that they are either all system and no passion or all passion and no system. Done correctly, CQP efforts strike the balance between the two through confident, informed leadership.

Attempts to treat quality as strictly rational reflect the beliefs of the post–World War II business curriculum. An entire generation of senior managers, many of whom Tom Peters once dubbed WOMs ("white older males"), was taught that the business world was a rational place. Emotions, they were advised, were something to use at home (and, even there, they were optional). In contrast, the quality movement led to a growing realization that emotions play an important role in the workplace, that organizations that wish to get ahead must deal with the fact that they have humans on their payroll, and that humans are marvelous mixtures of rational and emotional characteristics.

An instructive parallel can be expressed as a mathematical notation:

Leadership : Quality = Management : Productivity

In English, that indicates that the relationship between leadership and quality is equivalent to the relationship between management and productivity. The words can even be moved around—as with a mathematics formula—and remain true:

Leadership : Management = Quality : Productivity

This simple formula reflects the reality that leadership is both rational and emotional in nature, as is quality, and that management is solely rational, as is productivity. In other words, management is a subset of leadership in the same way that productivity is a subset of quality. This is hard for some executives to accept and difficult for most to adapt to.

Being a manager, being productive, is relatively straightforward and provides the comfort of formulae presented in various classes as being "sound" and "proven." In either productivity or management, textbooks are definitive: If a person does A and B, C will happen. People and machines are both considered to be functionally interchangeable and can be treated in much the same way to reach consistent results, results that will be predictable, even if suboptimal. And there's no question that the workplace would be less stressful if everyone functioned and reacted in the same identical, predictable, rational way, but that simply isn't the way the world operates. Or, at least it isn't the way the world operates when people are free to quit whenever they choose.

But until a person makes the leap from management to leadership by adding emotions—including humor and tact and caring—to his or her rational capabilities, the organization cannot step up from productivity to quality. Jim Kouzes, coauthor of *The Leadership Challenge* (1987), makes the point that "Emotional intelligence plus requisite experience has more value than IQ plus requisite experience." Not surprisingly, dealing with the emotional side of leadership isn't easy, but it is worth doing. Where management skills fall short, leadership skills can fill the gap.

Emotional/Rational Commitment

One encouraging note in the emotional/rational dichotomy is that progress can be made even before the full emotional commitment of all the senior managers is a reality. Intellectual assent, acknowledging that the pursuit of quality is a smart, worthwhile effort, is sufficient for a beginning. In fact, even with a fast start (or, perhaps, in part because of a fast start), it usually takes a while for a CQP to become a natural part of a company's operations. A CQP will be up and active and effective before everyone has bought in emotionally—although a critical mass (not necessarily a majority) of folks are needed to get it rolling. A critical mass has been reached when employees no longer feel like they are out there by themselves in their embrace of quality. It is a lot easier to be brave in a crowd than it is to lead the charge and be first.

Having both an emotional and a rational commitment from the CEO is ideal, but a basic structure to get the organization going down the correct path can be determined with a rational commitment from the majority of senior leadership. After studying other organizations' successes and understanding the potential impact on the bottom line, senior managers can give their assent to an approach to quality and agree to provide at least the minimum in the way of obvious support. Emotional commitment can come later. After all, for the CQO's very practical purposes, all that counts is the behavior of the senior executives, not what is hidden in their hearts.

While it isn't unusual for a rational commitment to a quality effort to precede emotional commitment for senior folks, individuals at the other end of the corporate ladder often begin with an emotional commitment as a result of realizing that "they," the senior managers, are going to trust them to make decisions and that "they," the employees, are going to have increased—perhaps dramatically increased—control over how to go about their day-to-day, hour-to-hour tasks. That's exciting stuff.

With the passage of time, as senior folks observe quality's impact on the corporation and on the individuals who make up the organization, more and more of them will become emotionally hooked. That's guaranteed. They will be pleased to have had a positive impact on the morale of those who work with and for them; they will feel the pride that comes from being a leader in an organization that keeps its promises and is competing well in the marketplace; and they may even get caught up in the fun that is an inevitable part of a process that includes a high degree of celebration and gratitude.

At the same time, the junior folks will acquire a growing degree of intellectual commitment. "This is wonderful," they'll acknowledge, "but how is our stock price doing? Are we really listening to our customers? What is the next evolutionary step in the growth of this process?"

When people at every rung on the corporate ladder are both intellectually and emotionally committed to the concept (the simple part) and the mechanics (the difficult part) of the quality process, continual improvement will be an integral part of the culture of the organization and a natural part of its mission.

The Implications of Trust

Under the heading of "truth in advertising" or "full disclosure," heed this warning: Trust in employees' abilities and goodwill is essential to a CQP. If a company engages all of its employees in the effort to improve everything, there will be so much simultaneous activity that it will be impossible to micromanage the implementation of ideas. Trust up front is an act of faith; trust over time is a matter of practical necessity. Intellectual agreement to launch a CQP opens the gate to a flood of activity that renders personal hesitations by senior managers moot.

At a workshop for a Baby Bell in the 1990s, the president of the company informed the authors of this book that "We can't trust our people." The stunned silence that greeted this pronouncement should have been a signal to him that his direct reports were not in complete agreement, but the remainder of the workshop was spent looking at ways to make his employees more trustworthy. With that attitude at the top, however, it was little wonder that morale problems plagued the organization. Clearly a change of heart (if not a personality transplant) on the president's part was called for before any quality effort stood a chance. And change of that kind is extremely trying and personal. It is axiomatic that the greater the change required of an individual, the more anxiety generated. But keep in mind: Only the self-confident can lead; insecure people can only manage.

For reasons not well understood, humans are better at trusting strangers than they are at trusting people they know. For instance, visualize the trip to the office of an all-too-typical American business executive. Having left home, the executive climbs into a car and immediately begins using the brake system—despite having no idea who personally assembled that brake system or what language they spoke while doing so. Each time the traffic light is green, the office-bound executive drives through, trusting people on the crossing streets to stop just because they happen to have a light of a different color shining at them.

Once at the office (and after, most likely, having parked next to the building in an "executive only" space), the executive rides an elevator to the executive floor—without ever looking to see who last inspected the elevator and guaranteed it would not crash into the basement. By the time the executive sits down at his or her desk, he or she has literally trusted his or her life to dozens, if not hundreds, of complete strangers—but now, safely behind an appropriately large desk, the executive routinely hesitates about trusting Chris with a $25 decision—despite the fact that Chris has been with the company for 27 years.

Picture another traffic scenario: You are at the wheel of your car, the twelfth or fifteenth car in line at a red light. You can see the light from where you are, but when it turns green you don't move. Why not? Obviously, everyone would like to see as many cars as possible make it safely through the intersection before the light turns back to red. Yet there you sit.

You stay where you are, of course, because the car in front of you hasn't moved yet . . . because that driver is waiting for the next car up the line to begin to move—and so on. Eventually, everybody does move in turn, and the farther back you are from the front, the more you have to hustle to try to make up lost ground: distance that was lost because you stayed still while others in front of you were moving. And not many actually make it through the light.

Now imagine if you and all of the drivers in front of you knew each other well enough to trust each others' responses. With that kind of relationship, when you saw the light turn green, you could move your foot from the brake pedal to the gas pedal because you would know that the same thing was happening in every car in front of you. All the vehicles could start up together. And as a result, more cars would get through the light.

What's this got to do with a CQP? The first case—when you waited until you were sure about what everybody in front of you was going to do because you didn't know them or trust them to do what was right— was what happens when the chain of command is populated with senior executives who micromanage. Nobody makes a move until they are certain of what the person in front of them is going to do. No one moves until the person who is next up the chain of command actually commits himself or herself to an action. No trust, no chance-taking, no risk . . . just slow, sure steps that will keep things looking neat and orderly, but that probably won't get you up to the light before it turns red again.

In the second case, one in which every driver knows that all of the other drivers are committed to a common goal (get as many cars through the light as possible) and are playing by the same rules (green means go), everyone can react simultaneously. But it takes trust and cooperation.

By extending trust to the employees of an organization, the senior management is playing the odds. The majority of the employees know their jobs and would never knowingly harm their organization. Remember, when they are at home or talking with friends, they usually refer to their place of work as "my company." The feeling of ownership reflected in that phrasing is real and can be relied on. At Paul Revere Insurance Group, of the first 25,000 implemented ideas, only 11 had to be undone after review by the quality analysts—and none of those ideas had been in place more than two days. Most management teams would rather have 24,989 ideas implemented in a timely fashion and put up with 11 short-term miscues than delay the 24,989 good ideas for undefined periods. Likewise, in the first four years of Quality First at the Insurance Center, none of the 8180 implemented ideas were reversed.

Pushing Authority Down

Trust is demonstrated through agreeing to useable guidelines prior to action. When calling on everyone on the payroll to contribute to the continual improvement of everything the company does, the senior leaders must ensure that they don't invite chaos by getting across the idea that everyone should attack whatever problem or challenge catches their eye. As a basic example, the folks in the mail center can't take on restructuring the vacation regulations. Nor should the folks in administration tackle rethinking the assembly line processes, even if they think it would be a more interesting and financially beneficial task than investigating their own procedures.

One way to help make guidelines clear is to introduce (and repeat and repeat and repeat) the definitions of responsibility, authority, and accountability. Responsibility is the obligation to act; authority is the power to act; and accountability is measuring and reporting the act and accepting the consequences. When authority and responsibility match, accountability is unambiguous, and you have empowerment.

But how do you determine responsibility? By seeing who is going to get blamed if something goes wrong. If a person or team does something exactly how they have been told to do it, and if someone else holds the power to make changes and the result is below expectations, the blame resides with the power-holder, not with the person or team doing the implementing. Or put more colloquially: "If you're going to get in trouble if it goes badly, then you have the authority to act to improve the outcome." Authority equal to responsibility: the definition of empowerment. If a person or group does not have both the responsibility and the authority to act, there can be no consequences, either positive or negative. Keeping track of what happens and making results known to everyone impacted by any changes are essential in any case, but accountability is always linked to authority.

Empowerment is the essence of delegating and the limits must be clear. Think of connecting four dots to make a box. You have a choice of writing instruments. When drawing the lines of authority—that is, when defining a person or a team's responsibilities and their limits for exercising authority—the instrument for drawing must be the equivalent of a no. 2 pencil, not a wide-stroke paintbrush. A wide-stroke paintbrush leaves a broad, wide line. It puts an area in question: The outside of the line creates one box and the inside of the line a smaller one. Does authority extend to the outside of the line or is the inside of the line the limit? Instead of clarifying the situation, a broad line just confuses it. That's simply counterproductive. Be sure to define the limits crisply.

Trust and leadership can, together, push authority down to the appropriate level. But how do authority and responsibility get out of sync in the first place? Ironically, authority is one of the few things in nature that drifts uphill over time. That is, responsibility and blame can remain at level A while authority moves up the corporate level in one of two ways.

In the first case, authority moves up when an employee moves up. Imagine someone was the best performer the company ever had at level A. That person's reward was, of course, promotion to level A + 1, a job filled with challenges about which this person didn't have a clue (at least not at first). The person's very natural reaction? To bring along one or more of his or her favorite projects, things that he or she does well and that often garnered praise for him or her while still at level A. These projects then become a part of his or her job at level A + 1, even after learning all the new stuff. And those same projects tend to remain at the new level even after the instigator moves to another job (or even another company).

The other common way for authority to drift to a higher level than responsibility occurs when an error is made and, rather than seize a teaching moment, the manager above the mistake-maker simply takes over the decision making. From then on, the responsibility remains at the lower level, but power has been moved up and added to what is probably already a pretty full agenda.

When a CQP effort is installed, assessment of current procedures and who exercises what power when often uncovers dozens of responsibility/authority anomalies. What happens then? Senior managers at every level have the opportunity to push power back down the corporate ladder, thus freeing up their time to do the jobs they are being paid to do, rather than making the often easier decisions that rightfully belong to their subordinates. If a manager works 40 hours a week and if he or she is spending only 10 percent of his or her time making decisions that should be being made at a lower rung of the corporate ladder (all of these decisions may well have migrated up the ladder long before the current office-holder moved in), then pushing those decisions back down to the appropriate, responsibility-bearing levels will free up four hours a week . . . a full half-day obtained "for free" to devote to doing the manager's appropriate job.

Looking at it from the employees' viewpoint, usurping power is damning. In a *Wall Street Journal* column titled "Overcontrolling Bosses Aren't Just Annoying; They're Also Inefficient" (March 30, 2005), Jared Sandberg lambastes managers who worry about the little stuff. "Deeply untrusting and puffed up with some devil-in-the-details justification, control freaks wrest tasks from colleagues, along with the colleagues' sense of self worth. . . . The irony is that in the name of efficiency and cost savings, these managers are often the most guilty of operating far below their pay scales." He quotes Richard Kilbury, senior director of the office of human services at Johns Hopkins University, as saying that these managers create a culture that tends to drive out creative people.

Middle managers who refuse to realign authority and responsibility and who—either quietly or actively—resist the disbursement of power required when implementing a Complete Quality Process, can slow the effort to a crawl or even a standstill. Fortunately, if these slow learners are in the minority, their lack of support for the corporate effort rapidly becomes evident because of the lack of progress in their areas compared to other areas in the company. Then it's time to take remedial action.

To empower others is an act of leadership. And it is worth repeating that leadership requires self-confidence. It requires a person not only to be sure of his or her own abilities, but also to be comfortable preparing subordinates to step up and accept the authority being offered. And preparing individuals for decision making entails an understanding of the fundamentals of leadership.

A Crash Course in Leadership

There remain people in corporate America who sincerely believe that leadership is an innate trait, that leaders are born and cannot be made. The position flies in the face of both history and common sense and reflects the idea that only a minority of people are capable of exercising leadership skills. In fact, leadership can be taught and it can be learned.

One of the richest possible benchmark sources for learning leadership is the military—either the American military or the military of any democracy in which individuals are assumed to have value. (See Appendix A for parallels between quality and productivity, leadership and management, and democracy and authoritarianism.) When the emphasis is on control, as it is in the ISO series, you can be sure that people are thought of in groups. It isn't surprising that few useful ideas about quality and leadership have come out of countries with basically socialist economies or nondemocratic governments.

This is not to say that, for maximum performance, all members of an organization should wear the same clothes, carry weapons, and walk side by side in straight lines. It is to say that that singular discipline—leadership—can be lifted out of the context of the military and dropped into a civilian organization with minimal adaptation necessary.

To demonstrate the point, take a look at these principles of leadership that are taught by the United States Marine Corps. Note that if the word "marines" in principle 3 is changed to "employees," the list is no longer military-specific:

1. Be technically and tactically proficient.

2. Know yourself and seek self-improvement.

3. Know your Marines and look out for their welfare.

4. Keep your personnel informed.

5. Set the example.

6. Ensure that the task is understood, supervised, and accomplished.

7. Train your people as a team.

8. Make sound and timely decisions.

9. Develop a sense of responsibility among subordinates.

10. Employ your command in accordance with its capabilities.

11. Seek responsibility and take responsibility for your actions and the actions of your unit.

These leadership principles describe what a leader does; they give guidelines both for personal behavior and for how to interact with subordinates—how to lead them.

Another important point to understand about leadership is the priorities of leadership. The first two of the following are from the military; the third was added by the authors of this book:

1. Accomplish the mission.

2. Take care of your people.

3. Create new leaders.

The first is done to get the organization through today. The second is done so that the members of the organization will get it through tomorrow. The third ensures that the organization will survive the passing of the current leadership team while continuing the legacy of the current leaders. Creating new leaders can be achieved throughout an organization: Leadership is a behavior, not a position. When anyone in an organization exercises authority responsibly, they are practicing leadership.

Another premise taught in the military is that there are three leadership styles: authoritarian, participative, and delegative. Agreement on the meaning of these terms is vital. Authoritarian leadership describes what occurs when one person has both the authority and responsibility. It is appropriate when three conditions are met:

- You have all the information needed to solve the problem.

- You are short on time.

- Your subordinates are motivated.

It should be noted that subordinates are only motivated when leaders practice participative and delegative leadership whenever possible. Participative leadership is often the most comfortable for both leader and led. It is appropriate when more than one party has pertinent information. The leader still makes the final decision and carries the responsibility for the decision. Delegative leadership is trickier. The leader retains ultimate responsibility for the decision—although the party he or she delegated to is responsible to him or her—but the authority to act is someone else's. It's been compared to someone saying, "Here's my career. Go play with it."

Information on other aspects of leadership, including mentoring, counseling, and leadership traits, are also offered in the texts from which the military teaches leadership. These government publications are available to the general public, and anyone interested in developing his or her leadership skills will find them a gold mine of information. Before leaving the topic here, perhaps the most important point to understand about leadership—and this too is lifted directly from the military—is that leadership is a subset of love. Grasping that hypothesis, one that deserves a good deal of thought and discussion, makes it possible for a person to become as effective a leader as his or her hard work and natural talents make it possible to be. Appendix B is an article—written in 1981 by one of the authors of this book—directly addressing the proposition that leadership is a subset of love. Although this view makes a large number of people uncomfortable, it can lead to very valuable insights into individuals and organizations when made a topic of discussion.

Setting the Example

Forget the tired phrase about how senior managers have to "walk the talk" and/or "talk the walk." The more accurate—and descriptive—phrase is that, when it comes to quality, the executives' hips and lips need to be moving in the same direction all the time. It is the responsibility of the president/CEO and his or her direct reports to set the example and to win commitment from the rest of the company. Quality needs long-term senior leadership involvement, not just a verbal commitment expressed from time to time.

Commitment to quality must, of course, extend to anyone who is seen as the boss—at every level. And it must be explicit. It is neither fair nor reasonable for a manager to assume that his or her subordinates are mind readers (or heart readers). Nor can a senior manager simply assume that once he or she "gets it" and makes a personal decision to join in the pursuit of quality, every single one of the middle managers who report to him or her will automatically make the same commitment. Middle managers need to be informed, courted, and led.

That's why commitment at every level has to be active, obvious, and informed. To have maximum impact, managers have to put their commitment on display. And in order to make one's participation obvious, it may be necessary to do what amounts to saying, "Hey! Look what I did." This may sound like bragging or blowing one's own horn, but it's better than leaving subordinates clueless about one's attitude toward quality. No one can follow an example that they don't see or know about.

One quick check on the involvement level of the senior managers is to ask, "Of the last 10 decisions that the senior managers made in the name of quality, in how many instances did the implementation of the idea require a change in behavior on the part of any of the senior managers?"

For the "informed" portion, an individual can dust off his or her old copy of *In Search of Excellence* by Tom Peters and Bob Waterman (1982)—or any other management classic that deals with quality or excellence or continual improvement. Better yet, he or she can keep an eye out for current articles having anything to do with continual improvement and share them with the other managers and subordinates. The bottom line is that bosses at every level have to be able to discuss the topic of quality with employees, either one-on-one or in groups of any size. Quality should be part of everyone's everyday conversation.

One of the most visible things that the Quality Steering Committee and the Quality Department can do is to define a program for recognition, gratitude, and celebration that requires senior management involvement. One such program is PEET, or Program for Ensuring Everybody's Thanked, designed as part of the CQP effort at Paul Revere Insurance Group in the early 1980s. It is presented both as a possible model for adaptation and/or adoption and to reinforce a point addressed earlier: that a person can do something effectively even though he or she has only given intellectual assent. In other words, form can come before substance.

The PEET Program

At Paul Revere Insurance Group at the beginning of their CQP effort Quality Has Value, the relationship between senior managers and the employee population could best be described as formal. It reflected a corporate culture in which ideas for change were conceived solely by senior managers. Fortunately, a few members of the upper tier of management realized that in an increasingly competitive marketplace, a difference in leadership style was called for.

While in the process of defining their quality effort in 1983, Paul Revere's Quality Steering Committee began looking for some way to teach executives how to "manage by wandering around"—the MBWA acronym that Tom Peters often admitted he'd lifted from Hewlett-Packard, but which became attached to his own name and legend. The response was the Program for Ensuring Everybody's Thanked (PEET).

After a couple of false starts, here is how PEET worked. At the beginning of each month, each of the 24 top company executives received a PEET Sheet bearing the names of two quality team leaders, a little bit about their teams' accomplishments, and their location and phone number. The executive's task was straightforward: Sometime during the upcoming month, he or she was to visit each of the two people on his or her PEET Sheet and talk with them. About anything.

There was a concern at first that people would balk at being visited by executives when the executive had been told to be there. That concern disappeared when the first executive to venture out of his office began his PEET visit with "Hi, I'm here to PEET you," and then explained what he meant. People, it turned out, didn't care *why* the executive was sitting by their desk talking with them; they cared only *that* the executive was there.

Initially, only a small percentage of the executives found time to make the visits. As a result, the company president, Aubrey K. Reid, announced that he had tasked the head of the quality effort (who produced the PEET Sheets each month) to follow up on who made visits. The upshot was a PEET Sheet Report, timed to arrive just before the monthly executive team meeting. Reid proved that he was serious about quality when, at the next meeting, he asked those executives who hadn't completed their two PEET visits to explain to all those present why they hadn't found the time.

As executives began making their visits, an interesting thing happened: They discovered that they truly enjoyed the unstructured time with the employees, and they learned a great deal about the people who made up their company. Visiting folks, listening to them, and learning from them became part of who the executives were and how they behaved, and corporate culture changed.

This is a dramatic example of how form—making the visits—can precede substance—change in how the executives and employees thought about each other. Anyone in an organization can do the "right thing" based on rational acceptance of an idea without being emotionally committed to it. Emotional buy-in can come second, after the behavior has already been initiated.

A Case Study in Leadership

At the UICI Insurance Center, where the relationship between management and nonmanagement was much more informal, the Quality Steering Committee decided to underscore the importance of leadership in the about-to-be-launched quality process in a different way. To create a common vocabulary and set of assumptions about leadership, they hired a training firm to conduct a series of three-day leadership seminars for no more than 30 people at a time. The senior management team went through the course first and then, over the space of a couple of months, everyone in the company at the level of supervisor or above took the class.

In addition to what was actually learned in the classes, there was tremendous value in the message conveyed. Both the supervisors—many of whom had never been sent to an off-site course before—and the rest of the employees were given tangible evidence of the company's commitment to leadership and quality: "Wow! This must be important! Look at the investment in time and money." Subsequently, the company had its internal trainers certified to teach the course so that classes could be conducted periodically. This enabled the Insurance Center to get newcomers up to speed on the thinking and vocabulary in the company and to offer refresher courses for those who had taken the course before.

Many members of the senior management team served on the Quality Steering Committee. All of them embraced Phil Myhra's mantra, "Mission, Quality, and Culture," publicly affirming both the importance of the quality effort and the role of a corporate culture in moving a company forward. The mantra also underlined the need for senior leadership to have clearly stated goals for themselves and for the company.

One of these individual goals was active participation on a quality team. Another was to take part in team recognition ceremonies. Yet another was to regularly show interest in the activities of all the teams in their area. And initially, many managers served as quality team leaders themselves.

Quality team leaders are, in fact, the heart of the Quality First process. At the Insurance Center, Myhra's—and, later, his successor Max Hill's—deep commitment to empowering and trusting the quality teams was integral to the success of the CQP. The "down in the trenches" leadership of the quality team leaders keeps Quality First going, day-in and day-out.

To borrow a phrase from the sales world, leading a quality team is "where the rubber meets the road." Finding times when most of their people can get together; letting everyone who is on the team and everyone who will be affected by the meeting know about it; nudging ideas and possible solutions out of team members who are not used to being asked to reevaluate what they've been told to do; directing all appropriate measures and experiments; getting ideas certified through a quality idea tracking program and database: All are new skills and all of them are acts of leadership.

Accepting the position of quality team leader takes a special kind of person: someone who cares about the people that he or she works with on a daily basis, someone who is willing to learn new ideas and techniques, someone who is willing to step up and risk being judged by others, someone who wants to improve his or her leadership skills, and someone who cares about the future of the company.

Personal leadership, the one-on-one or one-on-a-few leadership practiced by quality team leaders, is often the most difficult form of leadership because there is a chance of immediate disappointment when followers don't respond. But it can also be the most exciting form of leadership. Quality team leaders can be catalysts for change and improvement. But what kind of teams do they lead?

5 The Ins and Outs of Participation

A Complete Quality Process acknowledges the abilities of every person on the payroll and gives them the opportunity to effect change. That's a challenge. The organization has to create an environment in which people will be able to contribute to the improvement not just once, but repeatedly over the long haul. With this in mind, the senior management team at the Insurance Center agreed to a number of elements of 100 percent participation, subject to modification, during the four half-day classes in March 2000. The result was an ambitious agenda:

- Every employee of the organization would be enrolled in the process. The wording suggested was that participation in the process would be "nonvoluntary." (This avoided the use of the emotion-laden word *mandatory*.)

- The primary form of participation would be membership on a quality team.

- Quality teams would have approximately 8 to 12 members and, at least at first, the teams would be "natural work units" and the senior person would be the team leader (e.g., a supervisor would be the team leader for the team consisting of the folks who worked directly for him or her). This was expected to change over time as other people took their turns at being a leader and as teams became cross-departmental.

- Quality teams would have authority equal to their responsibility and would be allowed to implement ideas on their own say-so.

- Before a quality idea was officially recognized (the word *certified* was chosen), it would be checked by a member of the Quality Department.

- All certified ideas would be recognized with an appropriate thank-you.

- Efforts to improve overarching processes (in answer to the question "Are we even doing the right things?") would be conducted in parallel to the quality team efforts. The majority of the time, quality teams would address the question, "Are we doing things right?"

- The time frame for defining and implementing the process would be very compressed by normal standards.

One of the most important decisions made was that the quality teams would be nonvoluntary. If membership on a quality team were voluntary, a number of folks would elect not to join. Based on past experiences with quality efforts, the nonvolunteers might even mutter something about, "Been there, done that, fooled once, not twice." Past experience with a CQP led the chief quality officer to believe that at some point these holdouts were going to notice that folks around them—all those who did volunteer—had more control over their own work, had made their jobs more satisfying, were having more fun—and that management kept coming by and saying "thank you" and giving them gifts of various types.

When volunteering begins to look like a not-so-bad idea, however, a major problem arises: In order for this Chris-come-lately to get on a quality team, the first thing that he or she has to say is, "Ahh, I made a mistake. I'd like to join a team now." That sort of verbal self-flagellation is pretty unpopular with everybody. Rather than admit to being wrong, most folks will choose to stay in the "not a member" group. Nonvoluntary membership, however, makes it possible for someone who failed to contribute for weeks or even months to say, "Hey, I've got an idea." No barriers to climb over—other than possible remarks such as "It's about time" or "Welcome aboard" by teammates.

Beginning with the "nonvoluntary" decision, the Quality Steering Committee began hammering out the details. They decided that a *quality idea* was any change in procedures that saved time, saved money, improved customer service, or improved the work environment—without having an adverse impact on anyone else. Rather than train every person in the company prior to launching Quality First, the committee decided that only the team leaders would receive training on the theory and practice of quality, how to use basic measuring techniques, how to use the tracking program and database, and the theory and practice of leadership. And the committee outlined a system of recognition, gratitude, and celebration.

Looking at the agenda and the subsequent decisions, each point seems fairly straightforward, even uncomplicated. Any organization could make similar commitments. Any organization could form a Quality Steering Committee to adapt the basic CQP to their corporate culture. So why, after examining the list, would an organization resist doing so?

Too Ambitious for Us . . .

There are a number of reasons why an organization may choose not to adopt a CQP approach. Some companies already have quality control specialists (or productivity analysts) on the payroll and are content to hand over responsibility for quality to them. The quality control approach is normally restricted to catching errors that have already been made and stopping them from leaving the company. Americans old enough to have had their first experience buying a new American car prior to 1980 can remember a time when any knowledgeable person tried to find out exactly what day of the month a car had been assembled. The desirable vehicles, the ones that had the highest probability of being low-maintenance automobiles, were those put together on the first Wednesday of the month. Why that day? Because absenteeism was lowest mid-week and there was no push, early in the month, to meet production quotas by "getting them out the door" regardless of inspection failures.

This approach to quality has two major drawbacks: Given their numbers and the generally low regard in which quality control specialists were held, plenty of mistakes made it out the door. With quality by inspection (often followed by quality by direction—telling employees what to change and how), improvements may result, but the process won't win the hearts and minds of employees. Without the commitment of employees, no improvement is permanent.

Other organizations are headed by executives who are convinced that 100 percent participation is a fantasy: wonderful to contemplate, impossible to achieve. Most of these same executives, however, are willing to agree that something better than after-the-fact inspection is necessary to compete in an international marketplace. Hence the popularity of the Japanese Quality Control Circle initiatives and their cousin, focus groups. In both, the pursuit of quality is something that a person does in addition to his or her normal job. Participants choose to take part—and then only when invited to do so by the company. Oftentimes, becoming a participant in what were called quality circles in America was like signing up for a health care plan: Open enrollment was rare. And if that weren't enough, management retained the right to decide whether or not to implement the final results of the circles' hard work.

Whether the initial question was phrased, "Who should we assign?" or "Who do we think might be interested in doing this in addition to their real job?", it boils down to the same thing: "What subset of the company population will be counted on to improve the whole company?" Limiting participation holds a definite allure for executives, despite its shortcomings, because it is emotionally satisfying. Both quality control and quality circles leave control at the top and require little from the top management team beyond assent.

But assuming that 100 percent participation is possible, the question that sets an organization on the right path is, "Who can we afford to leave out?" And the answer certainly should be "Nobody." Letting everyone in on decision making, however, can be emotionally challenging to egos at the top of the corporate ladder. Virtually all executives are going to find out that people who earn a lot less money than they do and have had a lot less formal schooling than they have are going to have ideas that never occurred to them. Of course, if the senior managers can't muster the strength of ego needed to allow others to contribute to the improvement of the organization, they can refuse their help. And hope no stockholder or member of the board of directors ever asks why.

It really is that stark: How can any organization justify not trying to enlist the brainpower of everyone to whom it gives a paycheck? Why settle for the help of 20 employees when you can have the help of 200? Or the help of 400 when there are 4000 folks drawing paychecks? Rather than reviewing people (or units) one by one, hoping to find those employees with that special something, just admit that the Human Resources Department has been hiring adults and that everyone knows something about her or his job that no one else knows. It's about respect—respect given to the employees by the executives. The alternative, after all, is to say, "I think Human Resources has done a lousy job and hired lots of morons."

If, of course, an organization does have people on its payroll whose superiors believe will never have a useful or creative thought, there are other problems to solve before addressing an organization-wide approach to continual improvement. For example, it would be fair to ask, "Why is that person—whose boss now insists is a dolt even though that person has been here for eight years—even on our payroll?" Or "Why has that boss kept someone on the payroll for eight years—with no apparent attempt to improve matters—when he or she thinks the person is a dolt?" Keep in mind that just as people will often live up to high expectations, they will, at least as frequently, live down to low expectations.

Beware the Quality Purists

Recall Phil Myhra's mantra, "Mission, Quality, and Culture. Mission is what we do. Quality is how we do it. Culture is how we work together to get it done." In far too many organizations, quality has been introduced—or thought of—as one more task on top of all the others (see the discussion of quality circles in the previous section). Such an attitude, whether specifically introduced from the top of the corporate ladder or allowed to grow from the bottom up, cripples a quality process from the outset because it allows everyone to think of quality as an extracurricular activity, one that can be pushed aside at crunch time (see the discussion of quality control in the previous section). Quality must be understood to be an integral piece of how everyone's job is done.

Surprisingly, even after there is agreement that 100 percent participation is possible and desirable, the very fact that quality is defined as "how we do it" creates a new problem. Quality purists often express a vociferous objection to creating a structure to encourage and capture ideas for improvement. The chief quality officer should expect to find these purists both on the Quality Steering Committee and in the employee population as a whole. These are the folks who announce, usually loudly, "If everybody just did their job, there wouldn't be any need for a structure." The number and impact of the purists can be minimized by addressing the it's-just-their-job issue in this way:

Quality Department:	"You say it is their job. Were they doing it that way before?"
Purist:	"No."
Department:	"Are they doing it now?"
Purist:	"Yes."
Department:	"Is the company better off for having them do it this way?"
Purist:	"Yes."
Department:	"Then, let's say 'thank you' and make the change formal—and permanent."

The point is that whatever an employee got paid for last week is effectively his or her job description—not the formal write-up somewhere in the Human Resources Department. Recognition for making changes redefines the job—even when all it does is match performance to what was expected, but wasn't being done. Recognition also helps to ensure that any change becomes permanent. After all, what is important is that improvement has taken place.

That isn't to say that the it's-just-their-job argument is entirely without merit. As employees look at their jobs critically, they become more aware of what the company expects from them. They themselves raise the performance bar. But especially in the early stages of a CQP, a generous spirit helps to encourage employees to report ideas. Later, the definition of a quality idea can be more stringent, as employees become more sensitive to what their "real" jobs are.

Saying that quality is "how we do it" is a theoretical statement, a first step. But only practical mechanics, a day-to-day structure, make quality effective and bring benefits to the bottom line. Theory is both grand and necessary, but it doesn't actually "do" anything. On the other hand, the mechanics won't be much good, nor will they be sustained for long, if the theory isn't there as a foundation.

One caution: To be effective, an effort to draw on the knowledge of all employees needs to be less bureaucratic and more dynamic than many quality methodologies. The structure must be inclusive and easy to understand and use. It must be consistent—and capable of being modified when necessary. Achieving an improvement, and sustaining that achievement until another improvement is implemented, requires knowing what quality is and what role every person on the payroll plays in making the statement "Quality is how we do it" a reality.

Making "Quality is how we do it" more than just a slogan also requires something these authors call *creative discontent*. Employees aren't looking for ways to improve their jobs when everyone is happy; nor do employees feel they can improve things when everyone is unhappy, when the only thing that seems possible is to endure. Change, especially positive change, happens when folks are comfortable enough, but not satisfied. That's when they look for possibilities for improvement—as long as they know they can effectively change things. Creative discontent, discontent accompanied by questions and possible solutions, is the mother's milk of a quality process. Not sure what your quality team should look at next? That's easy: What annoys you in the workplace? What do you do that you are pretty sure is wasteful or, at the least, could be done better? What do you do that never seems to work out right the first time—or that always seems to leave your customers asking more questions? Start there. And when creative discontent becomes a habit, the result is a steady stream of ideas for improvement.

Creative discontent exists in every organization—it's just looking for an outlet. Lillian S. Murphy found hers by writing an article titled "The Anatomy of a Dictaphone" (*Supervision*, May 1975), in which she bemoaned time and money lost:

> Ironically, many big concerns proudly fly their suggestion boxes like a banner, little appreciating that it takes sheer guts for an employee to put her name to a totally bold or strong suggestion. Here, the company is definitely the loser, for if they could only get a sneak preview of behind-the-scenes activities from the transcriber's angle, much time and subsequent expense could be saved. . . .
>
> It's par for the course that most rules set down by many businesses are mostly launched by individuals who actually never come anywhere near handling or performing the routine duties for which they lay down the law.

Murphy devotes two pages to helpful hints for making transcribing more efficient and effective (see Appendix C), all things she'd like to tell her boss. The year was 1975.

A Case Study in Participation

The computer-based suggestion program that ran until the "real" quality process was initiated at the UICI Insurance Center was deliberately kept simple. Any employee in the company could submit an idea about anything. Within 24 hours, the CQO was at the employee's desk with an appropriately emblazoned coffee cup to give to him or her, along with a bunch of questions about exactly what was meant and what suggestions the person had for implementation. This gave the CQO the opportunity to meet a few hundred employees, as well as several dozen supervisors and managers, as he chased down possible solutions to the submitted suggestions.

The suggestion system not only introduced the word *quality* to the company vocabulary, it provided an opportunity to discuss the upcoming Quality First process. The communication and education accomplished were by themselves well worth the cost of some coffee cups plus a bit of the CQO's time. And although a suggestion system is essentially passive and subject to management approval (unlike the team approach the company was working toward), there were still 251 suggestions between April 15 and September 13, 2000. Fifty-two of the ideas were implemented.

Perhaps the easiest way to capture the general tone of what happened when the UICI Insurance Center switched from a suggestion system to quality teams is to look at several of the messages sent out to all employees. Early in the process, in addition to the personal campaigning done by the three members of the Quality Department, messages like this invited employees to take part in Quality First:

Mao Tse-Tung, the late founder and ruler of Communist China, left behind a lamentable legacy of death and suffering—but he is credited with one dandy quote: "A journey of a thousand miles starts with but a single step."

Now, he used the phrase to describe the persistence needed to sustain a revolutionary force as it began a long struggle to overcome the ruling bureaucracy and establish a new way of doing things. And, in fact, his forces literally did begin their campaign with a march of over 1000 miles. And they did eventually triumph.

But the phrase also applies to a quality process. You can't get "there" unless you leave "here." And you probably can't leave here easily or all at once. Small initial moves are more the norm, changes that test the system without incurring great risk for the people (or quality team) making the move. As quality ideas are put in place and the promise of empowerment is proven to be more than just pretty words, the pace and impact of quality ideas can accelerate.

But first, the journey from here to there—a journey that can look a thousand miles long when viewed from the starting point—must start with but a single idea.

Every quality team is urged to make that start. If a quality team leader needs help of any sort in getting his or her team out of the starting blocks, be sure to call the Quality Department to discuss your specific challenges.

A Whole New Year of Opportunities!

Another message sent out early in the process gave folks a new way to think about their quality challenges and, perhaps, a new way to explain them to somebody else:

In the movie *Groundhog Day*, Bill Murray had to relive February 2 again and again and again—until he finally got it right. Only then could he move on to February 3 and beyond.

It was a funny concept and a funny movie, but it is not the way life works for the rest of us. If we do something less than perfectly on January 1, for instance, it's still there, with all its problems and shortcomings, on January 2 . . . still waiting to be improved.

Instead of being able to count on a do-the-day-again-until-you-get-it-right loop to make it possible for us to continuously improve until we make things perfect, we have the Quality First process. It is our way of making things better today so that tomorrow will be easier and less frustrating. Granted, it requires more calendar days than Murray's system did before we get a particular process to work as well as it possibly can, but the Quality First process does make it possible to get the improvements made.

The trick just might be to take advantage of the tools and possibilities the Quality First process offers right away—and frequently. Murray, after all, had to live through an awful lot of Groundhog Days before he could finally move forward in time. Had he caught on more quickly, he could have gotten on with his life far sooner.

Don't let yourself be left doing the same inefficient, incorrect process again and again and again. Gather your quality team together and say, "Hey, I know how to get out of this cycle: I've got a quality idea!"

When, at long last, Murray did the right thing, he was quickly rewarded. Though the recognition, gratitude, and celebration that the Insurance Center puts forward isn't in the same category as that won by Murray (true love, being able to drive out of town, being able to move on to February 3, etc.), it is fairly generous.

Most important, you'll have done what Murray found to be so hard to do. You will have taken control of your own future.

When Will Someone Fix That?

Once the process was under way, the tone of the messages changed from being mostly of an encouraging nature to being more instructional in nature, such as the following:

Several of the quality ideas that were implemented by the quality teams that have been recognized over the last couple of weeks corrected long-standing problems. These were procedures that everyone had probably known for a long time were not the best way to do things but, at the same time, folks figured there must be a reason for doing it "like that." Or they just figured it was someone else's job to fix.

If some procedure seems odd to you, there are two possibilities :

1. You can just assume there must be a reason for doing it that way that no one has ever bothered to tell you—and just continue doing it that way, even though it annoys you every time.

2. You can ask why it is done the way it is.

If you do ask about the procedure that seems odd to you, there are two possibilities:

1. Someone will tell you why it is done that way and then you'll understand and your work will be less—probably much less—frustrating.

2. No one will have a good answer and it'll be a good time to change the procedure into one that makes sense.

If something doesn't make sense to you, it may well be because, even if it made sense years ago, it is no longer the best way to proceed. The worst thing that can happen if you ask is that you'll learn something useful.

Something just doesn't seem right—or smart? Ask.

Input and Output: Necessary to a Healthy Life

Once the CQP effort was rolling at the Insurance Center, this message went out:

For any living thing, there must be input and there must be output. That's true for the person or organization as a whole and it is true for each functioning component.

In our business, for instance, if the applications and premiums weren't coming in and the policies and payment checks weren't going out, everything would quickly grind to a halt. Within our company, each department—and each unit within each department—has input it expects to receive and output it intends to deliver.

For too many internal operations, input is delivered like the morning newspaper—it's left lying on their doorstep with no explanations and no interaction. Worse yet, when the receiving unit gets finished, it too frequently make a similarly uninformative transfer of its output to the next folks in line.

How to break the cycle? First, arrange a meeting with the folks who deliver stuff to you and ask, "What is this stuff, where do you get it, what do you do with it, and what do you think we do to it once we get it?"

Then flip the process and set up a meeting with the unit you pass your output to and ask, "Would you like to know where this came from and what we did to it—and what we think you are supposed to do to it? . . . And, by the way, what do you do with it?"

Among the things you are sure to find out are:

- There are some things you do very well (and spend considerable time doing) that are ignored, duplicated, or eliminated at the very next step;

- There are some things that you don't do, and everyone else has always wondered why you don't; and

- There are some things you do that repeat what the folks before you did.

A few conversations will save you a noticeable amount of work and greatly increase the quality of what you do.

Can't Be Done?

Humor was used to engage folks on both a rational and an emotional level. This message was once included in a Quality Newsletter:

When next someone says to you, "Oh, that can't be done," you might want to remember these true stories:

In 1881, when the New York YWCA announced typing lessons for women, vigorous protests were made on the grounds that the female constitution would break down under the strain.

When rayon was first put on the market, a committee appointed by silk manufacturers to study its possibilities declared it to be a transient fad.

In Germany, it was proven by experts that if trains went at the frightful speed of 15 miles an hour, blood would spurt from the travelers' noses and passengers would suffocate going through tunnels.

Catching the Big One!

Once the process gained momentum, some teams were implementing quality ideas with significant financial impact:

With most processes, results stay pretty much within a normal range. Folks who fish will tell you that most fish fall within predictable ranges of weight and length. Except . . . every once in a while . . . a big one comes along.

In this regard, quality is like fishing. Most quality ideas fall within predictable limits. As with the fish, the fact that they are predictable does not mean that they aren't important. They are, in fact, the lifeblood of the process. But . . . every once in a while . . . a big one comes along.

Quality Teams at the Insurance Center

In all of these messages, the meaning was clear: Employees were not only empowered to take action through their quality teams, they were expected to do so. Everyone, including the president/CEO, was on a team. The first year, the president/CEO and his direct reports split up and became members of teams made up of their subordinates, including, of course, the team leader. (The alternative would have been to form a team consisting entirely of the president/CEO and his or her direct reports.)

The Quality Steering Committee suggested that each quality team meet for 30 minutes each week. These meetings were to be presented and understood as time set aside for reflection about the job, a chance to think critically about how to change, to improve. In this theoretical world, the committee envisioned that the quality team leader would have a jam-packed agenda, and the team would have a spirited and productive discussion, deciding what it would work on in the coming days to improve various aspects of what the members do.

It didn't quite work out that way. But say that it had. One of the objections to a total team approach is "all that time in meetings." In the third year of the CQP effort at the UICI Insurance Center, the accumulated soft dollar savings were calculated to be $5,465,117. At $15 an hour, that means that 364,341 hours of work were eliminated—freeing up the associates to devote that time to tasks that really did need to be done. Imagine now that the 1150 associates had each spent two hours a month in "those meetings" (a rounded-up number). That would be an investment of 27,600 hours spent to achieve those savings. Return on investment? Over 13 to 1.

As it turned out, despite good intentions at all levels, it was not always possible to gather a majority of the team members in one place at one time for a nice, orderly meeting—especially on a regular basis. Employees spent far less time in meetings at the Insurance Center than anticipated—and still grasped the opportunity to make improvements. What follows is an approach recommended to the quality team leaders at the Insurance Center based on feedback after Quality First was launched:

Haven't got time to "Do quality" and your job? How about a "silent auction"?

There is so much going on at the Insurance Center that it is not unusual to hear someone say, "I haven't got time to 'do quality' and do my job!"

So then what happens? Particularly if you take into account the idea that quality is not something extra you do in addition to your job. Quality is how you do your job.

If there isn't time for formal quality meetings that tie up a dozen people at one time for 30–60 minutes, that doesn't mean that anyone should stop thinking about getting better. In fact, the time when we are overloaded is the most logical time to be thinking, "There has got to be a better way to do this" and to look for ways to begin the improvement process.

Can't do 10-person meetings? How about two-person and three-person meetings while walking down the hall?

Think of this like a live auction and a silent auction. The former is a large event that simultaneously takes the time of a lot of people. It is enjoyable to share the moment with others and a lot happens in an hour or more. A live auction can be compared to a quality team meeting: everybody is there at once, people quickly build on each other's ideas (bids), and people are inspired by the energy in the room to do things they might not normally do.

But there are also very successful silent auctions where people just write down their bids (ideas) and walk away—and then other people come along on their own schedules and add value to the original notation. Often, people will return again and again to see if anyone has added to what they last said/bid and, if appropriate, add even more themselves. Doesn't happen as quickly as a live auction and there's not as much energy and excitement and laughter. But it works quite well.

A team leader can either set up a large sheet of paper or have some e-mail address that all team members can get to and invite all team members to note any ideas they might have—even if incomplete—on one medium or the other. Whether or not they have an idea of their own, they should, when possible, take a look at their team's ideas lists and add any comments/value they might have.

What is important is that we all continue to improve what we do and how we do it—to make our own jobs more satisfying and more enjoyable and to better serve our many customers. There is more than one way to do this "quality thing."

Most quality teams ended up meeting on an ad hoc basis with discussion about improvement in groups of two or three or four—sometimes followed by an e-mail to the quality team leader.

Traditional team meetings or nontraditional ones, having everyone on a quality team greatly increased the odds that a person with an idea—big, small, or only partial—would tell someone else. Why? The person with the idea knew as a matter of simple fact that, no matter whom he or she was talking with, that individual was also engaged in the continual improvement of the organization. Teams also raised the odds that groups of people with partial ideas would encounter folks with the missing parts of their ideas. In other words, the chances of achieving a critical mass of knowledge was far better because some of the people may be holding their piece of the puzzle unknowingly—unaware that if their knowledge teamed with that of one or more other employees, a major breakthrough could occur.

Doing Things Right vs. Doing Right Things

Quality teams were only part of the approach to quality improvement at the Insurance Center. As stated in the agenda, the company wanted to address two questions: "Are we doing the right things?" and "Are we doing things right?"

The first question was the starting place for a look at an organization's basic processes. The question was if, with the passage of time since the processes were put in place, the company's work sequences actually were still designed to get the outcomes the company and its customers needed. It was a matter of looking, in a systematic way, at the methods that were habitually used to get things done. Too often, people and units do things the way they do them because it is the only way they have ever done them . . . and no one has ever told them to do it differently or given them the opportunity and/or the means to make changes.

Looking at work processes goes by several names, depending for the most part on which consultant a company contacts. Options include, but are not limited to, value analysis, process analysis, blueprinting, and lean. Each can be of benefit so long as it is kept in context. At both Paul Revere and the UICI Insurance Center, an outside consultant was brought in to lead the company's managers, department by department, through an investigation of what their objectives were and what their processes were—and, if the latter were well designed, to get them to the former. In the case of the Insurance Center, Candace Whelan of the Quality Department subsequently became the in-house process analysis expert. This was in keeping with best practices: Pay a consultant's prices in order to get things started expeditiously and then develop the skill in-house.

Because studying the company's procedures is primarily the job of management teams within each department and requires no prior training, examining work processes was started before the official launching of Quality First and the quality teams. The investment in managers' time and consultants' fees was one more reminder to the nonmanagement employees that the company was very serious about this quality thing.

Answering the question, "Are we doing things right?" is the shared responsibility of every person on the payroll. The primary tool for formulating answers and following through with those solutions at the Insurance Center became the quality teams, working with the quality analysts, both directly and through the quality idea tracking program and database. Earlier, less inclusive efforts at answering the "things right" question in American businesses included TQM, quality circles, and Kaizen. Experience with these approaches at other companies meant that some old-timers at the Insurance Center viewed quality teams as just one more fad to outlast. They were about to find out that they were wrong.

Gaining Momentum

As anticipated, not every person on a quality team was wildly enthusiastic at the outset. Some team members were exceedingly slow to buy in, as they waited to see what others were going to do to make their life easier. The senior management team had to wait and trust. Individuals and teams were given the opportunity to try this quality thing on for size, to talk about it, to try out a few small ideas, and to observe what happened to other folks. Initial meetings were a bit clumsy as team members found out that their ideas of what *participatory* and *empowerment* and *quality* really meant didn't square completely with what other folks (some senior to them, some not) thought.

A few quality teams, however, bought in immediately and started doing creative, helpful things. Some of the early ideas were so commonsensical that the initial reaction was often, "Are you sure we weren't doing it that way already?" As an indication of the way momentum built, the UICI Insurance Center had 557 quality ideas implemented and certified in Quality Year 1, more than double that number in Quality Year 2, and then more than double that year's total in

Quality Year 3. Idea totals didn't start leveling off until Quality Year 4—when there was "only" an increase of 40 percent over the previous year.

There are a variety of reasons why some people resist participating on a team. They range from past personal history with a failed "quality" program to hearing tales from a friend about a failed effort to personal caution about anything new to the simple fact that involving humans in anything comes with variability. The great truism is: Employees will become involved at different paces.

One explanation of the reasons why different quality teams and quality team members become active at different speeds was articulated at the Paul Revere Insurance Group in the mid-1980s. The first three stages were defined by Jeff Pym, who was responsible for the quality process efforts in the Canadian subsidiary, and the fourth was added a few years later by Robert McConville, the second person to run the quality effort at Paul Revere:

1. What can you do for me?

"Oh, good," the person at this level of commitment will say, "Fred (or Fred's unit) is going to stop making mistakes and that will make my life easier." The initiation of a quality process is welcomed by some because, perhaps at long last, the person or unit anticipates receiving trouble-free input. Most, but not all, folks will move through this level fairly quickly as they begin to realize that they are being offered the option to directly correct things that have bothered them for some time.

2. What can I do for me?

At this point, individuals and teams come to grips with the idea that they can take an active role in defining what they personally do for eight or more hours a day. Gaining some degree of control over what they do during a huge portion of their conscious hours gets some people very excited. And very busy for a prolonged time. Some individuals and teams will stay at this level for years.

3. What can I do for you?

Having gained sufficient control over their immediate environment and the ability to achieve their specifications, folks at this level have a greater degree of self-confidence and comfort in their workplace than they have ever had in a job before. At this point, they begin to reach out to customers to find out what they might do to help those customers—internal and external—meet their expectations.

4. What can we do together?

At this level, working, pragmatic partnerships form easily as quality teams and individuals search out new ways to work together to achieve organizational goals.

The progression through these stages is not entirely orderly. In fact, there is little in a CQP effort that is completely orderly. People don't neatly complete one level and then, without ever looking—or falling—back, move on to the next one. The more accurate observation would be that a quality team is *mostly* at a particular level. A team might, for instance, be mostly at the "What can I do for you?" level, but that doesn't prevent its members from devising a new way to answer, "What can I do for me?" or, for that matter, "What can we do together?" A CQP enables teams at all levels to move forward.

The most reassuring thing about team efforts to improve quality is that it is impossible for a team to run out of ideas. So long as the company keeps developing new products, so long as there is new hardware and software, so long as the number of customers grows, so long as management keeps reevaluating processes, quality teams will be faced with change. A Complete Quality Process gives the organization a way to keep up.

Changing the Process

For a process that calls on everyone else to change not to be open to change itself would be highly hypocritical. The CQO and the Quality Department must keep in mind that their responsibility is not to hold fast to some rules that once worked, but rather to promote the continual improvement of the company. One area that may be ripe for change over the years is the degree of toughness practiced by the quality analysts. As noted before, quality ideas that might have been accepted in the first year of the process—to encourage quality teams to keep thinking and to stretch their areas of investigation into more fruitful areas—might be turned down in subsequent years.

When Quality Year 5 began at the UICI Insurance Center in September 2004, the following Quality Team Leader Guidelines were published. The guidelines were discussed at team leader training and at team leader meetings and were posted on the quality idea tracking program and database. Please note that the tone of this message is considerably different than the initial messages to associates:

DEFINITION OF A QUALITY IDEA

A quality idea is an action that, when taken, changes an individual's or a team's job in such a way as to save time, save money, and/or enhance the business environment. While the idea improves the work environment and/or product of the quality team(s) or individual(s) implementing the idea, it must have a neutral or positive impact on all customers and on all other individuals or teams in the company.

ROLE OF THE QUALITY ANALYST

The primary role of the quality analyst is to verify and certify quality team accomplishments so that the improvements become a recognized part of work procedures and so that the quality team can be duly recognized. Calculations of costs and savings associated with a quality idea must be approved by a quality analyst. Assistance in these calculations is always available.

It is important to realize that some ideas may simply be judged as inconsequential by the quality analysts. Quality ideas that seem, in the judgment of the quality analysts, to have as their primary objective the adding of one more idea to the team's total, rather than any material improvement, are subject to disapproval.

TEAM INTENT

Teams must examine their intentions when considering the validity of ideas. The same idea applied to multiple areas may be valid in some circumstances and the team should receive appropriate credit. At other times, the idea may only be a minor correction or modification that is applied in multiple areas. It would be inappropriate for the team to take additional idea credits for a simple adjustment made in multiple areas based on the same idea. The team would, however, be able to claim the sum of any cost savings resulting from the adjustment being applied in many areas.

SHARING IDEAS

The sharing of an idea must be agreed upon, before implementation, by all teams involved and should be determined by each team's participation in the actual research/implementation of the idea. Each team will receive credit for an implemented idea, but the cost savings will be split among the teams (percentage of the split to be determined by the team leaders involved). Shared ideas must be implemented and certified during the same quality year. Quality ideas that have departmental approval and are submitted as BRs [Business Requests for a programming change] become part of the regular business workflow and are not subject to sharing with the work unit/team assigned to complete the implementation. If one team asks for information from another team and the information is readily available and does not require additional research/investigation, the team is not obligated to share the idea with the team who is the "owner" of the information.

If a quality team, inspired by an action taken by some other quality team, replicates that first team's idea, the idea can be counted as a separate quality idea (much like a shared idea) with nothing owed to the originator.

BUSINESS REQUESTS AND CERTIFICATION

A team will receive credit and cost savings for an idea requiring a BR when the idea is implemented and in production.

TEAM MEMBERSHIP

An associate can, in virtually all circumstances, only be a member of one team. Team members are always encouraged to support and assist other teams and to share their skills and experience. Some teams may be organized to focus on specific issues. Associates can be assigned to these "special issue" teams and still maintain membership on their original team.

Teams will be limited to a maximum of 12 members.

COST SAVINGS

Almost any good idea will result in time and/or money savings. Beginning in Quality Year 5, quality teams will be asked to begin calculating and documenting cost savings for *all* ideas. The Quality Department is always available to assist teams who may have difficulty determining the cost savings resulting from an idea. Occasionally, a good idea that enhances the workplace does not generate a cost savings and some ideas may even incur costs. The quality analysts will determine if it is either too difficult or impossible to calculate a cost savings for an idea.

Ideas with total cost savings of $50,000 or more are subject to review and approval by the department and the senior team. Because of this additional evaluation, the certification of these ideas my be delayed several days.

CONTRACT NEGOTIATIONS

Ideas related to contract negotiations will not be considered for certification.

PREMIUM DOLLARS

Cost savings related to premium dollars will be calculated at 10 percent. For example, a quality idea that results in $500,000 in annual premium will be assessed as having a one-time hard-dollar impact of $50,000 [the amount available for use elsewhere in the company].

TEAM LEADERS

Team leaders must complete team leader training. Team leader assistants must complete quality idea tracking system and database training. It is the responsibility of the team leader to obtain any required departmental approvals before implementing an idea. The team leader is also responsible for communicating any changes to processes, procedures, and/or workflows to any affected areas/departments. The team leader must be aware of the effect the change may have on other areas and act accordingly. Team leaders must ensure that all team member information in the database is current and accurate.

CONTRACTORS AND TEMPORARY EMPLOYEES

Contractors and temporary employees will not be able to participate in the Quality First process.

QUALITY IDEAS VERSUS "YOUR JOB"

In some cases, a quality idea may be considered a part of your job and not qualify for certification. The pivotal question is whether the improvement is one that is a to-be-expected outcome of your job or if the improvement is a change in a work process that is, essentially, added value.

As the CQP effort continues to unfold and flourish at the UICI Insurance Center, these definitions and guidelines will surely evolve in order to keep up with the creativity of the associates in the organization. That is one of the challenges. A quality process is not something that can be taken out of a box (or a book—even this one) and applied without changes. The effort to improve; the goodwill between folks at all levels of the organization; the search for new products and services, both internal and external: All of these will be constant factors, but the mechanics of the process must evolve.

6 Investing in the Future

Putting the requisite time and funding into a robust training program is difficult when an organization is caught up in multiple challenges, but Tom Peters' advice is still the best available on the subject: "If you are doing well, double your training budget. If you are not doing well, quadruple your training budget." Most companies provide orientation training and job-related training; fewer provide leadership training; and fewer still provide quality-related training. The success of a Complete Quality Process depends on a company being committed to providing training of all types. Whether the aim is to create a common vision or to increase competencies, training is an investment in the future.

One of the Teammates (a name chosen by popular vote in the company) at Ames Rubber Company shared a story at the Baldrige Quest Conference the year following the company's Baldrige win in 1993. A Teammate observed virtually identical charts on two adjacent desks. When he queried the residents of the desks about why they had the same chart, the three of them discovered that the charts represented two entirely different sets of data: One tracked expenditures for training and one tracked increases in productivity. Both were going steadily uphill. It was an intriguing, but not unexpected, parallel.

At the UICI Insurance Center, orientation training gives the company an opportunity to share its philosophy of quality, the vocabulary used throughout the company, and the day-to-day mechanics of the process. The company's approach to quality improvement is also incorporated into leadership training, but the main vehicle for transmitting quality values is the training given to quality team leaders. The curriculum of each of these courses, however, frequently overlaps to reinforce the substance of the concepts. The basic content of these curricula is covered in this chapter.

Getting Oriented

Even with the low turnover rate enjoyed by companies who have solid quality efforts (Ames had zero turnover the year they won the Baldrige), there are people joining the company every month—if only because the company is growing. It is an invitation to disaster to leave to chance the new employees' introduction to the company's habits of self-improvement. At the Insurance Center, the chief quality officer always takes part in orientation classes. His first question is invariably, "How many of you, in your previous work lives, worked for companies that had some sort of quality or productivity or continual improvement or excellence program—or something that sounds like that—in place while you were there?" Normally, somewhere between 50 and 75 percent of the folks in the room raise their hands. That's his cue to add, "Well, however your company went about it, we don't do it like that."

After a small ripple of nervous laughter, he takes the opportunity to lay out the basic premise at the Insurance Center: "In this company, the senior managers sincerely believe that Human Resources does its very best to hire adults. We'll be looking to you for ideas on how we can improve because you don't have our bad habits. As newcomers, you'll spot things that we won't. Point out things that don't make sense to you, and don't take 'That's the way we've always done it' as an answer. Quality is in your hands. That's what's different about the way we improve quality around here."

Much of the rest of the material for orientation classes is updated from material all employees received before the September 14 official birth date of the CQP effort. Everyone in the company was exposed to some "Here it comes" and "Here's what it is" orientation training, an hour or so in length. This was both informational and promotional, building up anticipation. It encompassed the rules, the structure, and the promise to the employees that this CQP effort would be around years from now—making it safe to get involved. It also included several important definitions, beginning with Quality in Fact and Quality in Perception. Understanding how the two interact enables employees to find ways to improve.

Quality in Fact is achieved and can be claimed when a person or unit meets its own specifications. When stated goals are met, when it can be demonstrated that what was defined as needed and appropriate has, in fact, been provided, Quality in Fact has been achieved. The problem, of course, is that Quality in Fact is not enough by itself. Just because a company makes something exactly as it sets out to do does not mean that anyone will voluntarily buy it. The Ford Edsel and New Coke illustrate the point.

Quality in Perception can be claimed when someone else (a customer) believes that what is being offered is precisely what he or she wants. The problem here becomes apparent when what the customer expects—and, very likely, based his or her purchase or acceptance on—is not what the provider actually made or provided. The resulting disappointment can eliminate further sales—or any kind of trust for years. Worse, customers tend to spread the word when they are dissatisfied.

Success comes when Quality in Fact and Quality in Perception are in sync. What the provider intends to provide, and does provide, must match what the customer is looking for. If it does, customers are happy—and potentially loyal.

But who is a customer? The simplest definition is anyone to whom you (and the "you" can mean you as an individual, you as a unit, or you as an organization) provide information, a service, or a product. That means a customer can be anyone from the person at the next desk to a money-providing consumer; there is no distinction between internal and external customers. Using these three definitions leads to the basic rule for quality improvement: Determine the customer's expectations—often by simply asking, "What precisely do you want?"—and compare those expectations to your specifications to see if they match.

There are two possible kinds of disconnect: specifications exceed customer expectations and customer expectations exceed specifications. If the provider's intentions exceed the customer's desires, the provider can either scale back the specifications (and save money) or maintain the specifications and try to convince customers that what is provided more truly meets their needs. This is very advantageous if it is impossible to obtain the particular better-than-hoped-for product or service from anyone else.

The other possibility is that the customer is looking for more than the provider is planning to offer. Again there are two theoretical choices: The provider can raise its specifications to match the expectations, or the provider can convince the customer that the lower specifications can meet his or her needs and will, indeed, be satisfactory. In the real world, what often happens is a compromise that begins with, "We can't quite do that for you, but let me tell you what we can do," and results in a combination of lowered expectations and heightened specifications.

Once the provider's specifications and the customer's expectations match, quality has been achieved. The next step? Wait a bit and then ask the customer again . . . because the expectations are going to change—usually upward thanks in part to what competitors make available and in part to people's natural inclination to think, "Well, if they can do this for me, I wonder what else they can do?"

Aligning specifications and expectations is only possible when both sides communicate with absolute clarity and both sides act in good faith. This is especially important for the provider. The slogan "The customer is always right" acknowledges that even when the customer is wrong, the provider suffers the consequences. Consider this example: Imagine that one bright Monday morning, you visit your doctor. "Give me something," you beg. "I have a big meeting in two days, and I have to be well enough to make a presentation." Unfortunately, your doctor is sympathetic, but not too encouraging, responding, "You have a bad cold. You're going to feel seedy for about five days. Try to get some rest and take this decongestant for the symptoms. That's the best I can do."

Not good enough. You call on another doctor and demand action. The second doctor barely looks at you and writes a prescription for antibiotics. You leave with the expectation that all will be well. Forty-eight hours pass and you stand to give your presentation. Your head is stuffed up. Your nose is runny. You feel awful—and you're mad.

Which doctor would you rather be? The one who told the truth that the customer didn't want to hear or the one who promised more than could be delivered? There is no doubt about your expectations as a customer: You wouldn't be truly satisfied unless you were well in two days. There is no doubt about the first doctor's specifications: No can do, but I can make you somewhat more comfortable. The second doctor promised to meet the specifications and (probably knowingly) fell short. Which doctor would you put your trust in in the future?

Establishing and publishing the rules and definitions of a CQP is one way that senior management can say, "Trust us." It can't be the only way, however, as trust is a major factor in this process and too many American employees are wary. It behooves the company to deliver the message in a number of ways: through actual classes conducted by senior managers, newsletters, posters—even the suggestion program described from the outset as a temporary alternative. Organizations can use anything that fits the culture of the organization.

Addendum to Leadership

Chapter 3 includes most of the leadership curriculum—with one notable exception. The CQO also put forth a 25-words-or-less definition of leadership that proved highly useful: "Leadership is the creation of an environment in which others can self-actualize in the process of completing the job." With that as a starting point, class discussion focused in large part on the question of how to create an environment to encourage folks to take control of their personal workplaces and to make improvements. The definition was instrumental in creating commitment to several components of a CQP: 100 percent participation, training, measurement, recognition, and communication.

Acknowledging a CQP as the environment in which employees' work can be done by making only minor modifications to the definition: "Leadership for quality is the creation of an environment in which others can self-actualize in the process of improving how they do their job." Why is this important? The opportunity to self-actualize means that employees are treated with respect, that their needs and desires are taken into consideration. One of the basic tenets of quality is that service to external customers will only rarely exceed service to internal customers. A blunter way of saying this is, "Nobody gives better than they get." Employees who are treated badly inside an organization should not be expected to turn around and treat an external customer with grace and good will. The few people who consistently give better service than they themselves receive are called *saints*.

It is no coincidence that every one of the MBNQA winners speaks at length about the need to listen to and support their own employees. Ritz-Carlton, the luxury hotel chain whose 1999 Baldrige Award was its second, has as its number-one corporate objective, "Improve the Pride and Joy and Satisfaction of All Employees." It is worth reiterating: In order for a CQP to succeed, the people in managerial roles throughout the company have to act as leaders—both by setting the example through their own involvement in the effort and by consciously (and obviously) working to create the environment that encourages their subordinates to grab this opportunity to take firmer control of their own workdays.

It Takes Teamwork

Before quality team leader training could take place at the Insurance Center, the Quality Steering Committee had to decide how to form the teams and how to choose quality team leaders. They took the logical approach and decided simply to mirror the organizational structure. If a person was, for instance, a supervisor with 10 or so people working for him or her, that person was made the quality team leader and the folks who worked *for* him or her become people who worked *with* him or her on a quality team. And so on, up and down the corporate wiring diagram.

Putting in such a mirror organization added a useful element of communications. Because all of the supervisors who worked for a particular manager were also on that manager's quality team, it became just a little easier to move potential quality ideas up or down the network to the place where the responsibility lay and where the authority should reside as well.

This was a good place to start because it was easy to understand and didn't represent a major, anxiety-producing shift in relationships. As people became more familiar and comfortable with the quality team option to getting things done, some teams recruited members from parts of the company who were their in-house customers or who held particular knowledge; some recruited members from vendors and out-of-company customers. Some team members elected to stay in the initial group. That meant that in some parts of the company, team leaders were always supervisors or other members of the formal hierarchy, while in other parts, the position of team leader became an informal audition for promotion.

The next decision was exactly who to train. The QSC asked a number of follow-up questions that set them on the right track:

- If there is a meeting of 10 people, how many of those 10 people need to know how to run a meeting?

- If there is a meeting of 10 people, how many of those 10 people need to know all of the intricacies of every or any form of measurement?

- If there is a meeting of 10 people, how many of those 10 people need to know the theoretical foundation of a quality effort and the mechanical aspects of the company's specific quality process?

The answer to each question is "one"—and quality team leader training was born. At the outset, one of the things that every quality team leader was made aware of was the absolute necessity of teaching his or her quality team members everything that he or she was being taught. This transfer of information was done on a whenever-you-can informal basis, either by example or by employing the information during problem solving.

The curriculum for Quality Team Leaders covered several main points:

1. How to run a meeting. This included both traditional meetings with all members sitting around a table with their agenda in front of them and the sort of meetings that became more common in a CQP effort: virtual or e-mail meetings, or meetings of two or three or four team members in a hallway or gathered around a desk. The principles were the same; the techniques varied considerably.

2. What is quality? This included the theory of quality in general, the reasons that the Insurance Center was making the investment to initiate and sustain a quality effort, and the type and extent of the impact that was expected.

3. One hundred percent employee involvement. That point made so much sense, many class attendees wondered why the point was being emphasized. The employees needed to know how special the CQP approach would be. (In refresher training, the idea of 100 percent employee involvement was introduced periodically—and the attendees were given a chance to congratulate themselves.)

4. How to use the day-to-day mechanics. This included information on what the procedures were going to be, including how to communicate with the Quality Department about the implementation and certification of quality ideas and details about the system for recognition, gratitude, and celebration.

No matter how well done the company-wide orientation effort and how complete the quality team leader training, not everyone will be interested in becoming active on their quality team. That's OK: It's another one of the "penalties" a company incurs when it hires humans beings. With humans, you get variety. Different folks will buy in, to different depths and at different speeds. All a company needs is a critical mass of folks who are willing to give the process a try. It doesn't even need to be a majority—just enough folks to make a big enough splash so that everyone else can see that (a) the ones who are giving this quality thing a try really are making decisions of their own about how to best do their own jobs, and (b) the company says "thank you" on a regular and generous basis.

What's a quality team leader to do with someone who mumbles, "Been there, tried that, got ignored"? An important part of team leader training is teaching team leaders how to deal with slow learners— how to keep them in the "we'll-listen-to-you-whenever-you're-ready" space, while not allowing them to bring down the whole team with their noncontributing attitude. The success of the team as a whole is the best assurance that eventually everyone will begin to take part.

A Word on Outside Vendors

It is quite possible that at the outset of a quality process, there will be no in-house capability for teaching the needed courses, beginning with the team leader training. If a company finds it necessary to use an outside vendor to help build the team leader course, it should insist on the following provisions in the contract with the vendor:

1. The vendor-built course will be customized to include all of the points listed in the previous section, plus any others the company feels are appropriate.

2. The vendor will include a "Train the Trainer" class in its pricing. The company's trainer(s) will then co-present the training to the first class of team leaders.

3. Once the company trainer feels comfortable teaching the class, the vendor will turn over all materials and allow the company to purchase complete in-house rights to the material. The company cannot, of course, peddle the class to any other corporate entity, but it can teach the course to its own employees as often as it likes and it can modify the course in any way it sees fit.

The reason for the third condition is that, after a course has been taught for a year, the company's Training Department (or the Quality Department folks who are doing this training) will have heard folks say things like, "You know, we've never used that one point," or "Gosh, I wish you'd spent more time on this point," or "Hey, I've got an example of that one point—because of something we did— that you might be able to use in class." Any of these comments or any variations of them can lead to fruitful changes in the teaching program and it should be possible to make those changes without asking the permission of the original vendor.

Incidentally, if a training company balks at these conditions, the company representatives should terminate the discussion. There are lots of good training vendors available and most of them will be happy to modify their standard contract.

Quality Training versus Job Training

Quality-specific training teaches folks how to go about the business of improving how they do their job, how to continually be on the watch for possible improvement, how to use measurement tools to determine what needs to be changed and in which direction, how to apply particular procedures when in search of the best way to implement an improvement, and how to work with others in such a way as to maximize the chances of continual improvement being the norm. Quality-specific training also includes leadership classes.

In the early 1990s, after being one of the first winners of the Baldrige Award, Motorola decided to make sure it wasn't going overboard on its quality-specific training. They hired an outside auditor to assess the cost of their quality-specific training versus its impact on their business. The results showed that the quality-specific training had a positive 30-to-1 return on investment.

Job-specific training, on the other hand, is focused on a particular set of technical skills and challenges. It is, quite simply, how to do the job according to the processes that are currently in place. As a quality effort takes root in a company, those processes will begin to change, and it will be the responsibility of the training unit to keep up with the current "way to do things here." The job-specific training must, of course, be continued, because it is impossible to improve a way to get from here to there unless you understand where the current "here" is and how to get to "there."

There is one great additional benefit that begins to build once a quality process is in place and having an impact. When turnover goes down because people don't want to leave organizations that treat them with respect, the time and effort that was being spent on orientation and basic courses can be reduced, freeing the company's trainers to spread their creative wings a bit and offer all manner of advanced training and nonstandard classes.

An example of this is advanced training in quality. Some quality teams will soon have gathered all of the low-hanging fruit in their area of the company and will be looking for more sophisticated tools to enable them to go after the more difficult challenges. The Quality Department folks will have to stay ahead of demand, which means upgrading their own skills. One of the strengths of a CQP approach is the freedom to accumulate a wide range of tools so that the right one can be available when it is needed. All of this, of course, means more training—more training to be attended by Quality Department personnel and more training to be given by Quality Department personnel.

One form of training put in place at the UICI Insurance Center was monthly team leader meetings. These gatherings were only 30 minutes long, but they gave the Quality Department the opportunity to keep the team leaders up to date on changes, to inform them of any upcoming training opportunities inside or outside of the company, to introduce some techniques and ideas for possible use, and to answer their questions. The meetings also gave the team leaders a chance to talk with and learn from each other.

The team leader meetings were both a formal learning opportunity and a much-needed support group for team leaders. Encouraging busy people to stop and think about possible improvements can be a tiring task; devising ways to measure and verify new processes can be daunting. Knowing that others are facing the same challenges and learning about the solutions they are trying can be a major boost.

The learning was two-sided. For one thing, the Quality Department found out which management folks were supportive—and which needed a nudge. They became aware of future training needs. And they learned how to continue to be effective in their role as the catalyst for the continual improvement of the Insurance Center.

Sad, but True . . .

There's a theory that if everyone in a company is trained in quality, progress will be accelerated. It's a nice theory, but the pragmatic reality is that it takes a great deal of time to complete a universal training program—and the incremental gain in group knowledge isn't worth the time or the expense. In fact, this approach has too often been a major contributor to a quality effort being stillborn. Companies that make an announcement to their employees and then embark on a prolonged preparation time engender skepticism. "Why," the employees will reasonably ask, "is this taking so long? Why don't they just ask me? I'll tell them what's wrong around here."

In the late 1980s, a phone company in New York made the "We're going to do quality" pronouncement and followed a consultant firm's advice that every single person on the payroll had to go through a week's worth of quality training. (Such an approach is known in the consulting business as "establishing a retirement fund"—for the consultant, that is.)

At any rate, the company spent over two years getting virtually every person on the payroll through the training. One of the authors of this book received a phone call from the company's quality director the day before the quality process was finally supposed to kick off. The quality director described everything that had taken place so far and then said, "It just doesn't feel right."

"Well," the response was, "let's say I went through your training, and I believed you. As a result, I came to work tomorrow with a neat idea for improvement. Where specifically do I go with that idea?" There was a long silence, followed by, "I think that's our problem." The process was abandoned within a year.

Quality teams answer the question, "Where do I go?" but leave a follow-up question, "What happens then?" The answer is simple: To turn a neat idea into a quality idea, apply measurement.

7 | Progress and Possibilities

S tart with this truism: Measurement is absolutely vital to improvement. How can you tell how far you've come if you don't know where you were in the first place? How can you talk about where you are without some objective standard? How can you plan to move forward if you can't figure out in which direction you're currently headed? That's what measurement is good for: checking progress and suggesting possibilities.

Problem solving is impossible without measurement, but it has to be applied in context. The quality community, by and large, misunderstood Dr. W. Edwards Deming. People looked at his degrees in things mathematical, focused on his call for the careful and thorough use of statistical tools, and assumed he was a measurement freak (or, more kindly, geek). Those who read his books more closely realized he was a humanist philosopher who believed that everyone should be given a chance to take part in improving their organization for reasons that owed everything to respect for the individual, and almost nothing to technical expertise. Measurement was certainly important to him, but his constant calls for treating employees with dignity had nothing to do with adding up columns of numbers. Yes, statistical process control (SPC) is important. No, it is not a cure-all.

One of the strengths of the Complete Quality Process approach is that it allows the introduction and use of all of the measurement tools that have been developed over the years in the name of quality. Is the function being investigated best looked into by utilizing Six Sigma tools? Fine. Use Six Sigma. SPC? That's good, too. But no single tool—not Six Sigma or SPC or any other tool—will solve all problems, especially if applied by a "traveling expert." It doesn't matter if the transient know-it-all is on the payroll or is an outside consultant who wanders into a department, demands piles of data, dictates changes, and then wanders off, measurement won't be effective until the people using it are convinced that there is something in it for them. Otherwise you're likely to find out the true meaning of lies, damn lies, and statistics: sloppy, misleading measurements are worse than no measurements at all.

When *measurement* is simply used as another word for *inspection* by an outsider who thinks in terms of pass/fail, a great deal of time and energy is bound to be wasted. When one of the authors of this book was a Marine second lieutenant stationed in Okinawa in 1964, his unit was scheduled for an inspection by the representatives of a senior command. While working with his Marines to clean up the work spaces in his unit, he discovered some excess gear—equipment that his Marines assured him they might need one day but that would count against them if the inspectors found it.

The lieutenant took the gear back to his BOQ room that noontime, intent on storing it under his bed until the inspection was over. As he began to put it in its temporary home, the Okinawan maid for that floor came by, saw what he was doing, and said, "Ahhh, so. Inspection come." The lieutenant's idea was not as original as he had assumed— and the inspectors probably knew the inspection provided a pro forma snapshot of the unit rather than a genuine one.

As is true with every other CQP component, measurement is both rational and emotional. Consider a case in which an employee is told by someone a few levels higher on the corporate ladder to take a particular measurement three times a day and to forward the results on a daily basis. Imagine now that two weeks have gone by and the manager arrives at the employee's work station, carefully recorded statistics in hand, and says, "Ah, ha! Now I know where the problem is. It's right here and these statistics prove it. You're the closest one to the source of the errors so you'd better get your act squared away right now or else." Given the manager's approach, the odds of getting any fruitful cooperation in the future are even lower than the odds of getting any accurate statistics in the future.

But imagine if the manager's statement were, "When will you be able to sit down and talk with me for a bit? I think I know where the problem we've been having might be coming from and, because you're the one who is closest to it, I'm betting you're in the best position to think of ideas on how we can fix things."

Same statistics. Same intent on the part of the manager. Essentially the same points covered in the manager's statement. The odds of immediate cooperation and continued accuracy in measurement have gone from near-zero to near-100 percent. The difference was not rational; it was emotional. Numbers are not rational or emotional; numbers are neutral. How they are used by humans is what counts.

Shortly after the launch of Quality First, Phil Myhra tackled the issue of measurement head on in a letter to every employee, most of whom were high school graduates. Printed on a piece of paper (reinforced by an e-mail) with a colorful banner headline in green and purple and posted on bulletin boards throughout the building, it took a meat-and-potatoes approach to the subject:

From the Desk of Phil Myhra, President

MEASUREMENT IS NOT JUST FOR MATH GEEKS

It has now been six months since we kicked off the quality team piece of our Quality First process at our first gathering at Birdville High School. During those six months, our quality teams have had a great deal of impact and almost everyone now has a better idea of what the challenges are to improve whatever it is they do.

Many problems have been solved, many improvements have been made—but many more opportunities await solution and require better tools, particularly measurement tools. I am convinced that if we are going to be able to take our quality efforts to the next plateau, we need better skills at measurement throughout the company.

But I also know that the idea of measurement puts a lot of people off. Plenty of folks think that in order to use measurement effectively, a person needs to be some sort of math geek.

The truth is that we all use measurement every day and that sometimes the measurements we use so comfortably are every bit as sophisticated as what is called for in the office.

Whenever you cook, for instance, there are a variety of measurements to be taken and monitored. When there are children in the house, you are often engaged in what can only be called competitive measuring about everything from the relative difficulty of household task assignments to allowances.

Sports fans, especially baseball fans, are overloaded with measurements and statistics and they understand and discuss them easily. The odds are very good that few measurements taken in the course of quality improvements will be more complicated to compute than the earned run average. But is that a number worth figuring? Absolutely— because it is a solid indication of the relative effectiveness and, thus, worth of a pitcher.

My point is only that measurement is an everyday thing and that folks should not be apprehensive about the fact that many supervisors and managers are going to "measurement school." They are not going to learn exotic and secret techniques. They are going to learn pragmatic ways to look at the work that they do and that the folks who work with them do and to reassess how to improve the procedures.

With the ideas and tools they learn, not only will they be able to take part in discussions about possible changes, they will be able to lead the discussion on how to determine exactly what is happening now and how to determine the precise impact of the change.

There are, after all, two valid uses for measurement in the context of a quality effort: (a) to determine data that can then be used as a source of ideas for improvement and (b) to check progress against expectations. If you are falling short of expectations, then you go back to (a) and use the data as a beginning point for more improvements.

With more measurement expertise in the company, we will be able to determine ever-more solid data—and we will be able to make improvements that are precisely on target. Using measurements well will give all of us even more control over our own work area.

Guesses usually aren't good enough in your personal life and they aren't going to be good enough here either. We are on our way to being the best health insurance company in the business—but we won't get there without a firm footing in measurement.

Thank you.

A Survey of Measurement

The MBNQA criteria are a valuable source of ideas for improving quality. In the process of answering the questions in the guidelines, organizations evaluate everything from leadership to strategic planning to human resources. The criteria are descriptive, not prescriptive, leaving room for innovation. They are also broader than those promulgated by ISO. When ISO first became accepted on a large scale in the United States, an in-depth study showed that their certification standards covered 10 percent of the material covered by the Baldrige. As the twenty-first century gets under way, it is estimated that a company could score 250 (out of 1000) on a Baldrige scale and be recognized as an ISO-certified organization. Fortunately, ISO standards continue to move closer to the Baldrige criteria with each evolution. Not too facetiously, it has been opined that after three more versions, the ISO office in Switzerland will be able to cut staff dramatically and forward their phones to the U.S. National Institute of Standards and Technology (NIST), home of the Baldrige. In any case, between the criteria and the well publicized experiences of the Baldrige winners, companies have a gold mine of ideas at their disposal.

In fact, quality has so many measurement tools at the ready that picking the right tool can be confusing. A quality process can include ISO 9000 (to fulfill a customer requirement, for instance) and/or reengineering (to rethink and redesign obsolete work processes, as was done with Quality First). Problem-solving options range from simple surveys and benchmarking (born from publicity following Xerox's Baldrige Award in 1990) to more complex SPC and Six Sigma (born from publicity following Motorola's 1988 Baldrige Award). As a rule, a senior management team in a CQP will need to decide how to address and solve three distinct types of problems: periodic, cyclical, and continual. Each provides its own challenges and is addressed by different measurement techniques.

Periodic problems, or one-time problems, occur as a result of specific, largely unrepeatable circumstances. These are best solved (much as they are in most organizations today) through the use of *task forces*—or whatever name the company has for groups that are formed to solve particular problems and that disband once the problem is solved. These quality SWAT teams are best made up of experienced problem-solvers in the habit of installing improvements. Of course, the company has experienced problem-solvers thanks to their involvement in the other two types of problems.

Cyclical problems deal with processes. Even the most basic of processes needs to be reviewed from time to time to ensure that the company is taking full advantage of changes that have taken place since the last review. These changes might be new tools the company has acquired or new demands and opportunities in the marketplace. Often these efforts are referred to as answering the question "Are we doing the right things?" and depend on some form of process analysis, value analysis, blueprinting, or reengineering to determine the answer.

Continual problems tend to deal with the question, "Are we doing things right?" This is the question most often associated with quality teams. It assumes that the higher levels of the organization have correctly defined the processes and objectives that were high-lighted through investigations of periodic and cyclical problems. The teams then ask, "Can we get there more efficiently? How can we further improve the process?"

Answering the question "Are we doing the right things?" can predate looking at "Are we doing things right?" The process analysis effort normally involves relatively senior folks, and perhaps only a few dozen at a time, as opposed to the 100 percent involvement that is a natural part of the quality team component—making it possible to initiate the needed workshops before all details are worked out for the CQP effort as a whole. Asking the question "Are we even built correctly to get where we want to go?" is one way to establish that the company is serious about improving quality.

Besides helping to build both momentum and anticipation, this also puts management folks in the lead, actually investing time and doing things that result in change for the better . . . in short, setting the example. It is possible, depending on how long it has been since the internal processes of the organization have been reviewed, for these efforts to be the catalyst for some fairly spectacular improvements. The quality team efforts that follow will produce a steady flow of relatively small improvements.

Quality teams at the UICI Insurance Center were encouraged to use the simplest measuring tools available, including surveys, benchmarking, and charting to look for opportunities to improve. A not-too-serious rule of thumb: "If you have to take a square root, you've gone too far."

Surveys can be an extraordinarily rich source of information and are, in theory, repercussion-free. The "in theory" caveat is added because there are a couple of rules you break at your peril. One is to never, ever ask a question unless you are prepared to do something about an answer you weren't expecting. Once you raise an issue, you must respond. In its simplest form, don't ask the employees if they like the color of the walls unless you are prepared to send someone to the paint store. Another rule is that, whenever possible, people should be told what the results of the survey were and what the department/company plans to do with the information. If, for instance, a person doesn't know that she or he is the only one who doesn't like the color of the walls, he or she might feel justified railing about the "unfeeling managers/imperialistic rascals who run this department/company and never listen to anyone." Knowing that he or she is in a minority of one holds the grumbling down. Just keep in mind that ignoring either rule breeds cynicism.

A survey that any manager can give at virtually any time—if he or she is prepared to follow the rules—can kick-start improvements.

The manager can gather all of the people who report directly to him or her and hand them each one page of paper that has only this written at the top:

The things that prevent me from doing my job better are:

The folks receiving the survey should be given at least a day to fill it out. Note that there is no signature line on the survey.

If the surveys all come back blank, the manager will know right away that one of two things is true: Either everything is perfect or he or she is not trusted—at all. If perfection is not the case, this is a clear signal that there is work to be done, even if not specifically on the unit's work processes. If, on the other hand, the unit is functioning well, the manager might see his or her name one or more times—still signaling work to be done. If the surveys come back with specific suggestions, the manager had better be ready to act on those that can be put in place and to explain openly why other points have to be either postponed or disregarded (probably for reasons that the person making the suggestion didn't know).

Benchmarking is another Baldrige-originated approach that can be used. It isn't as complicated as some experts would like to make it seem. Industry standards exist for many organizations and Baldrige winners are often willing to lend a hand. Looking at the task critically can also suggest unusual places to benchmark: The Red Cross benchmarked the dairy industry's procedures for moving milk in investigating transporting blood safely. Both Airbus and Boeing copied Toyota to speed up their assembly lines.

To understand how complicated benchmarking isn't, think back to Sleeping Beauty, the evil Stepmother Queen, and the Magic Mirror. The Magic Mirror was one heckuva benchmarking device. The Stepmother Queen could check her relative beauty simply by asking the Mirror. Of course, when she got an unexpected answer, she overreacted rather badly.

Imagine if she had used her benchmarking device more adroitly. Years before she finally got the "bad" answer, she should have been asking, "Is anyone almost as beautiful as I am? Is anyone gaining on me?" If she knew that someone else was getting closer each year, she may have been able to take some preventative steps or, when the bad news did arrive, she could have asked, "How do I compare beauty-wise to ladies in the neighboring countries?" and, if she was number one there, she could have essentially gone into export.

Measurement does, indubitably, make folks wary. Most employees are convinced that it takes great expertise. Yet, at the UICI Insurance Center, led by John Fynn and Candace Whelan (bolstered by various classes), quality team leaders at all levels of the organization routinely complete detailed measurements to determine what changes are needed and what impact they have.

It's Not for Me . . .

Resistance to the use of measurement can take many forms, but two arguments seem to have universal appeal. The first is, "You can't really measure what I do," and the second, "Perfection is impossible." Both of these statements are fundamentally untrue. While there may not be measurements in place to describe someone's job, and while deciding what measurements are relevant may be difficult, it doesn't follow that the task is impossible. If you suggest that the only logical thing to do in order to save money when no measurements are available is to cut the person's salary in half, you can be sure that the individual will cooperate in finding measurements that count.

As for perfection, achieving zero errors is possible at least some of the time and, as an intellectual construct, perfection is invaluable. Ask the question, "How many babies is it OK to drop in the delivery room?" and perfection as a goal seems completely reasonable. Bank of America ran an ad campaign that illuminated the way to perfection: It isn't a matter of doing a billion things right, it's a matter of doing a single thing right a billion times.

It might help the unconvinced to picture a person named Chris who works at the main plant of Company ABC and whose workday has just come to an end. It's time to drive home. Chris will get into his car and drive to the end of the company driveway and be faced with a decision: turn left or turn right or go straight ahead? Throughout the drive home, Chris will routinely handle dozens, perhaps hundreds, of decisions, and unless every decision is handled without error, the drive home is going to be frustrating and time-consuming. If Chris needs a carton of milk or a six-pack of something a bit stronger, putting in a today-only alteration to the travel plan will require something out of the ordinary. If circumstances, say a bridge being out for repairs, force longer-term alterations to be incorporated, Chris has to deal with that, too.

Taking all of that into consideration, how many times in a lifetime would Chris do a perfect job of getting home? Probably 100 percent. Chris is fully capable of executing a detailed sequence of events, including on-the-spot adjustments, perfectly over an extended period of time, even though the process is a complicated one calling for numerous decisions and judgment calls.

Why is this level of perfection possible? Because Chris understands the value of doing it right, has personal control over how things unfold, and is personally impacted by the results of the decisions. In the case of desired changes, Chris is able to make the decisions on how to effect these changes and when to revert to the original sequence. Just as important, when a better way is discovered, Chris has the power to permanently alter the sequence.

Chris is capable of perfection outside of the office building. Given the same level of involvement, understanding, and control, there's no reason Chris couldn't be just as perfect inside the building—to the organization's benefit. But neither Chris nor anyone else is going to strive for perfection if the price for making a well-intentioned stumble is punishment. People must be allowed room to fall forward. Good-faith mistakes have to be viewed as teaching opportunities; repeated mistakes do not.

Uniquely CQP

The Complete Quality Process at the UICI Insurance Center uses a measurement called *quality ideas* to determine "Are we doing things right?" in quality improvement. As noted before, quality ideas are implemented by quality teams working in their area of responsibility and authority. The definition of a quality idea is deliberately generous: any change in procedures that saves time, saves money, improves customer service, or improves the work environment—without having an adverse impact on anyone else. Sometimes a quality idea isn't particularly revolutionary and, perhaps, should have been done all along, but the emphasis is on where the team is now—not where someone thinks it should have been. If the answer to the following two questions is "yes," it is a quality idea: Is where you are now an improvement over where you were? Was the vehicle for getting from there to here an idea that a quality team member suggested and the team decided was a good idea? That leaves one question to be answered: Where does a quality team go with a quality idea?

With that in mind, a quality idea tracking program and database was designed as a means to elicit, evaluate, refine, and encourage the implementation of quality ideas, and as the primary communications link between the quality team leaders and the quality analysts in the Quality Department. The Insurance Center had a head start in designing the program because of the Chief Quality Officer's previous work at Paul Revere Insurance Group. Piggy-backing off the earlier program, Quality Analyst John Fynn worked with the IT Department at the Insurance Center to design an even better program, and the result was ready in time for the launching of the process in mid-September 2000.

After that program had been in use for a year or more, Fynn began working with the IT Department to develop a far more sophisticated—but still easy to use—program that made its debut in 2003. This computer program, or one like it, is essential to a CQP format. Like the process as a whole, it is simple in concept but can be difficult to build depending on the amount of detail desired. The heart of the program is making it possible for quality teams to log their ideas and enter discussions with the quality analysts about implementation and certification—and, of course, tabulating results. Beyond that, any organization can decide how much the program will also be used as a bulletin board for information about the process.

The quality idea tracking program and database is accessible both in the technical sense of the word and in the everyday can-I-use-it sense of the word. It makes possible the accumulation of knowledge in a retrievable manner so that it can be shared. Stealing ideas is actively encouraged. The primary function of the program is, however, to make it possible for the quality analysts to confirm calculations and certify ideas in a timely manner. The sequence is this:

- When a quality team has an idea for improvement, the team leader can enter the idea in the tracking program with whatever level of detail he or she feels is appropriate or, quite simply, has available. There is a "status code" entry to be filled in and, for an idea that is just in the thinking stage, a "1" is appropriate.

- If the quality team later decides to put the idea aside for the time being, they have the option of changing the status to "2" as a signal to anyone else that, although they think it is an idea worth looking at, they are not planning to pursue it at this time. The "2" status can also be used by the quality analysts as a way to put on hold an idea that a team says they have completed but that the analyst says requires further research and/or documentation.

- A status of "3" means the team has no intention of pursuing the idea. The idea is maintained on the database for other teams to look at and may serve as a starting place for someone else.

- When an idea is implemented—that is, the idea is in place and functioning—the team leader changes the status to "4." That is the signal to the quality analysts that the work has been done and certification is sought. For most ideas, this is the first time a quality analyst will get involved. All quality team leaders know that they can seek out the help of a quality analyst at any time during the development and implementation of an idea, but in most cases, using the measurement tools they have been taught and drawing from the experience of folks who do the task, manage the task, and/or are impacted by the task, the quality teams move to implementation on their own say-so, using the empowerment formula of "authority equal to responsibility." If an idea is initiated by one team but impacts or requires the cooperation of other individuals, quality teams, work units, or departments, it is the responsibility of the team leader to ensure that all cooperation has been put in place prior to making the idea a "4."

- Team leaders don't assign a "5" to an idea. In fact, a good tracking program won't allow them that option. A "5" means the quality analyst has reviewed the idea, confirmed all calculations, determined that the calculations chosen are appropriate and complete, determined that the idea will bring some improvement to the procedures of the quality team while not negatively impacting anyone else, and confirmed all needed approvals and promises of cooperation. At that point, the quality idea is not only implemented (i.e., given a status of "4" by the team leader) but certified (i.e., given a status of "5" by the quality analyst). Only when an idea is certified does it become "part of the way we do things around here," and only when it is certified does the quality team become eligible for any recognition.

As is obvious, the quality analysts are the linchpins of the successful day-to-day operation of a CQP effort. In addition to their central duty of working with team leaders on the development and implementation of quality ideas, the quality analysts' roles in the company continuously evolve and expand over the years. To add to their personal knowledge, both quality analysts at the Insurance Center became examiners for the Texas Quality Award (one of the 40-plus Baldrige-clone awards offered by various states). Fynn's computer skills led to his becoming a primary communicator within the company. Whelan discovered she had skills in the areas of process analysis and mentoring that were a boon to the company. Both proved to be marvelous at creating, planning, and producing company-wide celebration events. But always, their ability to work with team leaders, their understanding of what the quality teams were doing, and their ability to ask the right questions about the potential impact of an idea were vital to the success of the process.

Measuring Success

The results of the CQP at the Insurance Center through the first four years are a testament to its success. The quality idea tracking program and database captured the number of certified ideas and the savings both in hard dollars (money not expended) and soft dollars (capacity for work):

Quality year	Certified ideas	Hard-dollars savings	Soft-dollars savings
One (09/14/00–09/13/01)	557	$2,049,535.81	$3,366,450.31
Two (09/14/01–09/13/02)	1206	$3,482,014.73	$4,049,275.45
Three (09/14/02–09/13/03)	2709	$3,754,972.13	$5,465,117.30
Four (09/14/03–09/13/04)	3708	$9,198,186.41	$8,301,155.39

Though the fifth year of Quality First is incomplete, there had been 1654 certified ideas in the first eight months, with a hard-dollar impact of $1,260,364.46 and a soft-dollar impact of $1,876,292.43. Enthusiasm for the CQP hasn't waned through changes in leadership (by comparison, there were 1584 certified ideas in the first eight months of Quality Year 4) and a major acquisition that introduced a new product. Quality teams remain up to the challenge of revisiting "Are we doing things right?" when the right things are altered.

Once a quality process has been well defined and well implemented, it will, with encouragement in the way of giving people responsibility and authority and extending gratitude, take on a life of its own. And why should it slow down? So long as the company keeps developing new products, so long as it keeps getting new hardware and software, so long as there are new customers, and so long as management keeps reevaluating processes, there is no reason for it to slow down. Quality teams are just keeping up.

At the UICI Insurance Center, Quality Year 5 officially began on Monday, September 27, 2004, when the quality idea tracking program and database was turned on (i.e., made available after some maintenance). As in past years, all the teams' counters were reset to zero. By the end of the day, one quality team had already made it to the first level of recognition with five certified quality ideas with a soft-dollar value of $12,832.75. Seven other teams had 13 additional ideas that totaled $3,964.58 in soft dollars and $15,701.75 in hard dollars.

To quote a manager at Paul Revere Insurance Group, "If the president of the company were to declare today that the quality process here was being shut down, it would take about two years to kill it. People really like making decisions and controlling their own workplace."

8 Celebrate Good Times!

The UICI Insurance Center's program for recognition, gratitude, and celebration is an important aspect of its corporate culture. It adds an element of humanness and fun to the Complete Quality Process focus on incremental improvement by providing intermediate goals, saying "thank you," and finding unusual ways to communicate strategic goals. It's the way the organization builds a bridge between the rational and emotional aspects of quality improvement and it strengthens the relationship between senior management and the other 90-plus percent of the payroll. And it takes nothing for granted: Recognition, gratitude, and celebration are systematic, and it takes hard work on the part of senior management and the Quality Department.

The heart of the component is saying "thank you" to employees for quality improvements. The dollar savings and increase in capacity for work engendered by quality ideas at the Insurance Center are impressive, but it doesn't stop there. These improvements demand recognition from senior management if the company wants more of them. Imagine a nine-year-old the morning after a gift-receiving occasion (birthday, Christmas, whatever), sitting at the kitchen table with a stack of stationery in front of him or her and with Mother standing there with a list in her hand. It is obvious that it is time to write thank-you notes. Even Aunt Hazel must be thanked for those atrocious pajamas. Why?

As countless mothers have explained, Aunt Hazel is a sweet little lady who went out of her way to send those pajamas and, in return, she deserves to be thanked; she deserves the feeling of being thanked. That's the emotional reason. The rational reason is self-serving: If Aunt Hazel feels thanked, if she "hears" the thank-you, the odds are good that she'll send something again next year . . . and it might well be better than pajamas. Although the thank-you is to the giver's advantage, it is not necessarily cynical—so long as it strengthens a real mutual regard with Aunt Hazel.

So, too, in business. The company thanks its employees for their contributions to the continual improvement of the organization because (1) the employees have earned the feeling that comes with being appreciated, and (2) if the employees "hear" the thank-you, the odds are good that they will continue to help the company improve. And each side will be aware of the other in a positive way.

The problem is that different people hear "thank you" in different ways. The sign of gratitude, the gift, the particular prize given to one employee that causes her or him to feel warm and toasty inside might cause the second employee to wonder, "What's this thing for?" and the third employee may simply fall asleep. A program of recognition, gratitude, and celebration has to take this into account in order to be successful.

In too many organizations, the gift *du jour* is determined by whatever the person defining the gifts likes. If for instance, the president of the company—or the head of the quality process—really likes plaques, handing out plaques might quickly become a gratitude ritual. Now imagine that Chris and Pat have each done something pretty terrific. So the president of the company personally presents each of them with a suitably engraved plaque. At the end of the day, the president of the company might feel very pleased with the way the day went—to include taking time to personally present the two plaques. The transmission was great.

That night, in the sanctity of their own homes, Chris and Pat are both busy with their plaques. Chris's freshly polished plaque is going above the fireplace; Pat's is going *into* the fireplace. Reception was, well, uneven.

For some folks, the gift that really means something is money: "You give me cash; I understand that you are grateful." For others, a cash gift is greeted with, "Of course you should give me money— I'm underpaid. Now, how are you going to say 'thank you'?" What turns some folks on is the physical gift (with or without the company logo) that serves as a constant reminder that they did something well and that the company noticed. Others dismiss the gift as "another trinket"—no matter what its cost. And for still others, it is the fact that the recognition is delivered in person by senior managers that seals the deal. As with communications, it is reception that counts. How many times "thank you" is said is only academically interesting. What is important for the future of the company is how many times it is heard.

The recognition system that is built to be a part of the CQP effort must be obvious and easy to understand and it must be, at the initial stages, easy enough to beat so that most quality teams will be able to take part. It must not be perceived as an incentive (no percentage of money saved, for example) and it must be perceived as fair. At Paul Revere and again at UICI, there were two possible ways for a team to earn recognition: by the sheer number of quality ideas implemented and certified or by the total annualized monetary value of any number of certified quality ideas. Teams made up of folks from Human Resources, for instance, often earn recognition through a series of small improvements, while IT-based teams more frequently earn recognition through dollar impact. This eliminates another potential pitfall: No one (and no team) wins at anyone else's expense. Each team is judged and recognized based solely on what it accomplishes. No one misses out on being recognized and thanked because of someone else's actions.

In the following table, the recognition schedule used for Quality Year 4 (September 14, 2003 through September 13, 2004) at the UICI Insurance Center is spelled out. This schedule was always available on the quality idea tracking program and database so that everyone was able to see where they were and what was within reach. There were changes made every year, but never any huge overhauls.

In the first column is the name of the award level. When the process began in September 2000, the system was defined through Quintuple Gold, and additional levels were added as needed each year. "Ideas" refers to the number of certified quality ideas and "Savings" refers to the total hard-dollar and soft-dollar savings credited to the team because of certified ideas. A team achieves a level either through the appropriate number of ideas or the appropriate amount of financial impact.

As is evident, the gifts were clearly a thank-you and not an incentive. The gift check in the first year was for one of several area businesses. In the second year, the UICI Insurance Center began using American Express gift checks, accepting the fee as an expense attached to saying "thank you." "Bronze gift" refers to a collection of 10–15 items, each of which cost about $10 and has a Quality First logo. The other gifts are as their name implies—and each of them has a Quality First logo as well. Except for team meal awards, each award is given to every individual on the quality team.

Award level	Ideas or savings	Awards
Bronze	10 or $10,000	One Bronze gift
Silver	15 or $25,000	$25 gift check
Gold	20 or $50,000	$50 gift check
Double Gold	30 or $100,000	One Bronze gift and $50 gift check
Triple Gold	40 or $150,000	One Bronze gift and $50 gift check
Quadruple Gold	50 or $200,000	Catered lunch for team and $50 gift check
Quintuple Gold	60 or $250,000	Barbecue set and $50 gift check
Sextuple Gold	70 or $300,000	CD player and $50 gift check
Septuple Gold	80 or $350,000	Auto emergency kit and $50 gift check
Octuple Gold	90 or $400,000	Lunch with the department head and $50 gift check
Nontuple Gold	100 or $450,000	Travel garment bag and $50 gift check
Decituple Gold	110 or $500,000	Travel cooler and $50 gift check
Platinum I	130 or $600,000	Wine case, Dinner coupons for two, and $100 gift check
Platinum II	150 or $700,000	Picnic blanket, dinner coupons for two, and $100 gift check
Platinum III	170 or $800,000	Sport chair, dinner coupons for two, and $100 gift check
Platinum IV	190 or $900,000	Carry-all bag, dinner coupons for two, and $100 gift check
Diamond Plus	230 or $1,100,000	Team trophy, jean shirt, $100 Hickory Farms certificate, and $200 gift check
Double Diamond	270 or $1,300,000	Team trophy, picnic basket, dinner with company leaders (each member brings one guest), and $200 gift check
Triple Diamond	310 or $1,500,000	Team trophy, jacket, $100 Omaha Steaks certificate, and $200 gift check
Quadruple Diamond	350 or $1,700,000	Team trophy, beach towel, $100 certificate to a local sporting goods store, and $200 gift check

The Problem—and Challenge

Every recognition program must be prevented from becoming seen as an entitlement, something that is expected no matter what the contribution or effort on the part of the recipient. This will be a matter of continually explaining and repeating the basis for recognition and ensuring that, when given, it is always deserved. And it helps if the Quality Department leaves itself room to surprise people. In addition to the basically predictable and widely advertised forms of recognition, organizations should include irregular awards—irregular in the sense that they are given as surprises for actions or ideas because of their originality or unique impact.

An example of a one-time irregular award was a program conducted at Paul Revere in February 1989 called "A Cactus for a Thank You." The Quality Department discovered that a local discount department store would sell them small potted cactus plants by the dozen for a very reasonable (well, cheap) price. Because one of the lessons the company wanted to emphasize was the importance of thanking someone else and of doing something so well that someone would thank *you*, the small cactus plants were used as the gimmick for teaching the lesson.

The rules were simple. For February only, if an employee received a thank-you note from anybody for any job-related thing they did, all they had to do was bring a copy of the note to the Quality Department and they could trade it in for a cactus plant. On each little green, plastic container, the Quality Department placed a sticker that declared, "I'm Stuck On Quality." Corny? Yes. Popular? Yes, very much so.

So popular, in fact, that some people cheated and arranged to trade thank-you notes with each other so that they could each get a cactus and quit being teased by fellow workers for not having done anything that earned a thank-you. When a couple of quality purists reported the cheaters, the reaction was, "Let's say what you say is true. The fact remains that each of them had to think about something the other had done for them that was worth saying "thank you" for. End result: They each appreciate the other a bit more, they each know the other noticed something good they did for them, and it only cost the company two small cactus plants to strengthen the working relationship between those two. A bargain."

Why cactus plants? Because it was February in New England.

Impact on Senior Management

One aspect of saying "thank you" is inviolate: Senior managers must actively participate. Anyone who wonders "What's in it for me?" if he or she takes the time and invests the effort in saying "thank you" to the folks who work with and for him or her should consider these personal benefits:

- Growth toward being a leader

- Gaining a reputation for commitment to CQP with seniors and subordinates

- Making a positive connection with subordinates

- Increased knowledge of the capabilities of subordinates

- Enjoyment of his or her time on this planet

That last point may not be self-evident, but saying "thank you" is fun and it provides a stress-free oasis in the middle of a pressure-packed day.

From a hard-headed business perspective, one of the bonus results from involving senior leaders in a vigorous program of recognition is the education of those senior folks about who is actually doing what inside their company. It is a fair statement that the senior management teams of companies with CQP efforts know their organizations far better than those in non-CQP companies.

In the context of a CQP effort, recognition is most often accomplished in small, 10–15-minute ceremonies in which quality teams receive the gifts appropriate to their most recently attained level of achievement from a group that includes as many senior managers as possible. Phil Myhra, when he was president of the Insurance Center, attended virtually every ceremony during the first years of the Quality First process; when Max Hill took over as president in early 2004, he became an almost-every-time attendee. Other senior managers, members of the Quality Steering Committee, and members of the Quality Department were always on hand.

Before the distribution of the awards and the applause and congratulations, the quality team leader is always asked to "brag to us." Sometimes the task of bragging is delegated by the team leader to a specific team member who was personally involved in a particular idea, but either way, several members of the senior management team and Quality Department get to hear who is doing the really interesting and innovative stuff.

When the senior leadership of a CQP-practicing company receives requests for promotions or for budget adjustments, they actually know who is doing the recommending and who is being recommended for advancement. They know which managers and directors and vice presidents are encouraging their people to think and which departments obviously encourage innovation.

And . . . the Bottom Line

People who feel appreciated stay longer at an organization and work harder while they are there. Among the many studies that have verified this is "Rethinking Rewards," an article in the *Harvard Business Review* (November–December 1993). The authors of the article found that the primary motivations for employees are (in decreasing order of importance):

1. A sense of accomplishment in performing the work itself

2. Recognition from peers and top management

3. Career advancement

4. Management support

5. Salary

A CQP process easily bolsters numbers 1, 2, and 4 and, in the sense of giving employees a chance to showcase their talents for their bosses, can be argued to give a hand with number 3 as well.

Celebrations

The full title of this CQP component is "Recognition, Gratitude, and Celebration." Recognition is the name for the public acknowledgment of work well done. Gratitude, in this context, is the feeling the individuals have as a result of being recognized; as explained earlier in the chapter, the goal is to have every member of a quality team walk away from a recognition ceremony feeling as if he or she has personally been thanked. And celebration takes many forms.

The quality team recognition ceremonies are themselves small celebrations as team members' achievements are recalled and the team members applauded. When levels of recognition that include team meals are reached, that lunch or dinner gathering often takes on the aspect of a party. (In fact, food has been proven to be a relatively easy, and virtually always well received, form of recognition and celebration—as attested to regularly by Baldrige winners.) Broadcasting congratulations—through the use of universal e-mail messages, plasma screen displays in common areas, or various posters—is also done in a celebratory manner.

And there are big ones. When all the quality teams have been formed, the quality idea tracking program and database has been checked and double-checked, communications systems are in place, quality team leaders have been trained, the recognition system has been defined, and the leaders at the top are ready, it is time to launch the process. The occasion needs to be memorable—memorable enough so that in the months and years to come, people will still talk about how and when the process started, how and when the company began to change.

At the UICI Insurance Center, the launch of the Quality First process took place on September 14, 2000. Held at the 850-seat auditorium of the nearby high school, the Quality Kick-Off included a welcoming salute by the high school's marching band and an assortment of speakers—members of the senior management team, each of them given limited time. The repeated messages were, "This is the future of the company" and "This is something we are very capable of doing." The company promoted the idea that the Insurance Center was intent on making innovation intentional—in the sense that getting better, thinking of new ways to solve both old challenges and new ones, was to become "the way we do things around here." Creativity, the employees were told, is like a muscle: You must use it or lose it.

This was only the first of the big, all-employee events held at the high school. The Quality Department is responsible for two such events each year. One is the spring presentation of the strategic plan to all employees. Though more educational than celebratory, the presentation is also entertaining. When a company explains its strategic plan by making it into a musical production, there is, at the least, some fun involved. Students in the theater program at the high school help with the lighting and staging of these shows—and are thanked with gift certificates to a local mall. On one occasion when Myhra was giving the students their gift certificates, he asked them, "Is this what you expected corporate America to be like?" One young lady's answer was, "I sure hope so!"

The September anniversary celebration of Quality First is the second annual event. Called WeROQ—an acronym for "We Recognize Our Quality"—this is a combination entertainment and awards event with a different theme each year. At the end of Quality Year 4, for instance, playing on the homonym "rock," the 90-minute event featured a rock band and, for everyone in the company, a tie-dyed T-shirt.

Everyone was invited to the football stadium to sit on the grass, listen to guest speakers, and hang out Woodstock-style. The T-shirts are still being worn throughout the company nine months later.

No matter what the theme, the core of each WeROQ celebration is honoring the quality teams who achieved the largest totals in the past year, in terms of both the number of certified ideas and annualized dollars. In addition, special Spirit of Quality awards are given to teams with certified ideas that, regardless of their financial impact, simply demonstrated what the whole process is all about. To top it off, one or more individuals who have been particularly visible in their support of the process are given life-sized cardboard Oscars for being "Best Supporting."

As vehicles for morale-boosting and for emphasizing important points, the big celebrations have proven to be well worth the investment in time, energy, and money. No matter the size, all celebrations give speakers the opportunity to remind everyone why the company is pursuing quality: bottom-line impact, greater customer satisfaction, and happier employees. (There isn't an employee at the Insurance Center who hasn't heard the Ritz-Carlton quote, "Profit is the residue of quality," at least once.) Employees need to be reminded frequently that the quality effort is one of the most important ways the organization has to get—or stay—competitive in the marketplace. A CQP, done well, means the organization will have a future, and celebrations are the time to renew commitment.

Punny, Isn't It?

Being playful, enjoying work, is a hallmark of a corporate culture in which trust is paramount, and all the fun in a Complete Quality Process isn't generated at the top. For undefined reasons, virtually every quality process in an American organization has a fairly serious name, but quality teams (or quality circles or any other grouping) tend toward fairly light-hearted names. The quality process at Paul Revere Insurance Group, for instance, was named "Quality Has Value"—both a statement of belief and a signal that the intention was to pursue quality teams and value analysis simultaneously. At the Froedtert Lutheran Memorial Hospital, their effort (an early form of CQP) was named "QUEST"— Quality Underscores Every Single Task. And at the UICI Insurance Center, "Quality First" referred to the primacy of quality both as a goal and as a means to that goal.

In contrast, quality teams at the UICI Insurance Center named their teams with a lavish use of puns and humor: Acct Up, Check Mates, Close Encounters of the Premium Kind, Quality Divas, Rat Pack, H "R" Us, Problem Busters, X Files, and 12 Girls and a Guy. When the gentleman on that last team transferred to another department in the company, the all-female team renamed itself 12 Girls Re-Mastered.

When employees have the confidence to let their personalities show through, the organization can be sure that senior managers have done a good job of communicating that individual differences are accepted and valued. It's tangible evidence of management's shift in attitude from paternalism/maternalism—where employees are treated as children when they are at work and subordinates act like children and wait for specific instructions—to an environment in which adults interact. Quality teams make it possible for employees to bring their adult personas to work—including their sense of humor—and everybody benefits.

9 As I Was Saying . . .

Throughout this book, there have been samples of the messages put forth by the UICI Insurance Center Quality Department and top management. The written word is a powerful means of communication, but communication takes place in many ways. Senior managers communicate their commitment to a Complete Quality Process through membership on teams and through matching authority and responsibility in their departments. Training communicates skills and attitudes, as do recognition and celebrations. Body language, fighting fair, listening with a third ear, two-way/one-way/all-sorts-of-ways: Like the language that is a vital aspect of communication, the concept itself has been parsed in countless ways. What is often overlooked is that the totality of communication within a company becomes the corporate culture or, as Phil Myhra put it, "how we work together to get it done." That's why communication is listed as one of the components of a CQP.

There is no doubt that communication is complicated. That's not too surprising when you consider that it underpins every relationship. Interestingly, the number of people involved isn't necessarily a definitive factor. Think of all of the divorces based on a failure to communicate when there were usually just two people involved. Misunderstanding can take place in groups both large and small. Every organization involved in a CQP, however, can increase the odds of communicating clearly by paying attention to two narrow areas of concern: the idea of listening down and the intersecting roles of transmission and reception.

It is important to note that promoting the ideas of transmission versus reception and listening down does not constitute an attempt to change who anyone is. Rather, they are ways of changing how individuals go about presenting themselves to those around them and, thus, how people perceive them. Consciously adding options for how a person goes about his or her day-to-day interaction with the world affects a person in his or her job, making him or her a more effective leader. Leaders don't assume that people can read their minds. Leaders don't only talk to people when there are problems. Leaders communicate. Frequently. To all of their people. If you don't tell people what you think, you invite them to decide for themselves what you think—and they'll probably get it wrong.

Listening Down

Especially important to a CQP is a concept that can best be termed *listening down*. The all-too-common communication flow in a hierarchy of any sort is listening up. Folks at all levels of the organization are comfortable with the idea that those at the top of the chain of command will proclaim down to people on lower rungs of the corporate ladder. Such a procedure assumes that knowledge in an organization is cumulative as one rises in the hierarchy, so that everyone at level $X + 2$ knows everything that the folks at level $X + 1$ know plus some additional facts and, further, that the folks at level $X + 3$ know all that is known at $X + 2$ and more. Under the assumption that knowledge is stored in neat gradations, the communication flow is easy to understand and predict: It goes down the hierarchy as the people at each level seek to teach and/or direct the folks at the next lower level—who only have to listen.

The premise is, of course, nonsense. The problem is that few people ever actually think through the implications of what they are passively supporting. Worse, most people who take part in proclaiming down and listening up are usually pretty sure that he or she is the exception, that he or she should be listened to by those on the levels above, that he or she should be invited to proclaim up.

The truth of the matter is that folks at all sorts of levels within the company know all sorts of things that folks at other levels, higher and lower, have never even thought of. Managers at all levels must develop the habit of listening down and inviting subordinates to proclaim up. The recognition ceremonies described in Chapter 8 are one example of establishing a specific program to help managers develop this habit; paying attention to the input on the quality idea tracking program and database is another. Quality ideas are a way to train employees to proclaim up useful information.

What happens when an organization actively listens down is that the corporate culture changes radically. Once employees work in an organization where their ideas are taken seriously and they are treated with respect, they find it difficult to work in a less supportive environment. Make no mistake: This has an impact not only on keeping employees, but also on recruiting them. According to Erin White in a *Wall Street Journal* article titled, "Savviest Job Hunters Research the Cultures of Potential Employers" (March 29, 2005), "Culture clash is one of the biggest reasons that new hires fail." New employees often find a CQP corporate culture a delightful surprise.

Transmission and Reception

Clear communication also depends on recognizing the difference between transmission and reception. The first is the act of attempting to send—by any means—a piece of information to another person or to a group of people; the second is the act on the part of the intended recipient(s) of receiving and trying to understand the message.

To demonstrate which of the two is more critical, consider the case of Pete, a young Army captain who announced to his best friend Freida, another Army captain, that he, Pete, was about to be promoted to major ahead of schedule. Freida knew and liked Pete, but she knew that the chances of Pete being promoted early were small— at best. So Freida asked Pete, "Gosh, what makes you say that?" Pete's answer was, "The colonel told me," to which Freida replied, "What exactly did the colonel say?" "Well," Pete bragged, "he said that if I kept performing like I've been performing, I wouldn't be a captain for much longer."

The colonel may have thought he was being simultaneously disapproving and clever when he made his remark, but he left too much room for interpretation. Although there was no doubt in the colonel's mind that if Pete didn't shape up and improve his level of performance, he was going to be demoted to lieutenant, Pete isn't going to change his behavior based on the colonel's remark. Because of what he *heard*, Pete *knows* in his heart and in his mind that the colonel told him he was on his way to an early promotion to major.

So which is more important: transmission or reception? If the objective is to get something done, reception is. People react to what they hear, not to what someone else is very sure she or he said. Perception and understanding are built on what is heard; reception determines the beliefs of the recipients and becomes the basis for action. What is said or intended by the transmitter is only academically interesting.

When Alexander Haig, in the wake of the shooting of President Reagan, famously said, "I'm in charge here," what was heard was certainly not what he intended in the way of a no-reason-to-panic message, and it ended a possible political career before it ever got started. He was perceived as arrogant and overreaching. No one wanted to hear his explanation. What counted was what had been heard and understood—not what Haig intended to convey.

How do you go about ensuring that your message gets through within a CQP effort? By every means possible. The simple truth is that different folks hear things in different ways, just as different folks hear "thank you" in different ways. Some folks will take the time to read the quality newsletters and the notes from the president. Others will ignore them as too much bother, muttering "Same old same old." Some will respond to short, quick notes—perhaps delivered through all-company e-mails. Others take on board messages that are more visual than verbal. For them, posters or displays on plasma screens placed throughout an organization set up a situation wherein transmission and reception are the same.

How does a would-be transmitter of a message ensure that reception equals the intended transmission? By asking such questions as, "Would you please 'read that back to me'?" or "What did you understand from that letter I sent out to everyone yesterday?" This follow-up questioning can take the form of everything from one-on-one conversations to surveys. And, of course, all of the impersonal message-sending must be backed up by personal communication, whenever a senior manager is one-on-one with a subordinate or when he or she is talking with groups, large or small.

Sending a message about the quality effort in several different ways may seem repetitious to the sender, but because each receiver most likely only actually hears the message one or two ways, it is not repetitious as far as the audience is concerned. There is one basic message that must be consistently transmitted: Quality is how we do things around here and it will be that way until the walls come tumbling down, because it is the best possible thing for all of us individually as well as for the organization.

Samples of messages sent during the first five years of Quality First demonstrate how this message was reinforced again and again, giving details of day-to-day operations, discussing the philosophy of quality, linking quality to corporate culture. Each message addresses a single issue, but all of them echo or expand on the role of quality at the UICI Insurance Center.

Introducing Quality

Following is one of the messages sent to all UICI Insurance Center employees during the period of process definition between the informed decision to proceed (March 25, 2000) and the kickoff celebration (September 14, 2000). It laid the groundwork for quality teams:

"Quality is the lubricant that makes it possible for all of the parts of the organization to work smoothly with each other." That explanation of a quality effort by Phil Myhra captures the essence of why the Insurance Center has started down the path toward the definition and implementation of a company-wide quality process.

Put another way, quality is not something extra; it is not one more thing to do in addition to everything else we are already responsible for. It is, rather, how we do what we do.

The process being instituted at the Insurance Center is to be based on a simple concept: the belief that the Insurance Center is made up of a great number of responsible adults who would rather do things well—given a choice or even a chance.

Through a combination of individual training (primarily of quality team leaders at first) and system-wide support and recognition programs, everyone will be given the chance to make their own job, and the jobs of their teammates, more satisfying as well as to improve the efficiency and effectiveness of the organization: to "do things right." At the same time, a series of program management projects will ensure that the company "does the right things."

The primary difference between our quality process and those at the majority of organizations in America is this strong belief in the capability of every person on the payroll to contribute.

Where most attempts at quality begin with the question, "Who should we involve in this process?" we are beginning with the question, "Who can we afford to exclude?" The answer, of course, is "No one." Every person on the payroll is capable of improvement and original, creative ideas—if we are able to define and implement a process that makes it possible.

That's why every person will be formally involved in the Insurance Center quality process when it officially begins this fall.

What's in It for Me?

One of the most vexing questions when starting a Complete Quality Process is, "What's in it for me?" The following three messages were sent to the associates at the UICI Insurance Center during the period shortly before the actual initiation of the process. The messages were designed to both inform and reassure: to inform people about some of the theory and mechanics of the upcoming Quality First process, and to reassure them about the intent and the opportunities open to them:

WIIFM 1

Over the last several months, you have most likely heard at least one senior manager talk about quality. You may have called the Quality-Fone at extension 8438. You might have looked through an issue or two of the *I See Quality* newsletter that has been included in the *Grapevine* for the last few months. It's even possible that you're one of the more than 100 employees who have earned one of the "Quality on the Fast Track" coffee cups or noticed one on the desk of a friend. And you couldn't have missed the growing number of signs on the walls announcing the Quality First process.

All of which leads to a very logical thought: So what? What benefit is all this quality stuff to you?

Good question. Well, actually, two good questions.

This is the first of three short all-employee messages designed to try to answer the question "WIIFM?"—or "What's in it for me?"

First of all, you should know that every employee of the Insurance Center and the Applications & Solutions Team will be a member of a quality team—and, thus, be involved to some degree in the Quality First process. There's a reason for that: The organization as a whole and the senior leadership team in particular strongly believe that every person on the payroll is very capable of contributing to the continual improvement of the organization, particularly if they are given the proper tools and support.

Yes, but WIIFM?

A secure future. A quality process is a collection of various efforts to improve everything about the organization on a continual basis. In a world in which competition is often just a few mouse-clicks away, getting better and staying better means more than just profits, it means company survival. Every idea you have for improvement and every idea that someone else has and that you help to put in place helps to ensure the company's future.

On a more personal level, the Quality First process extends to each individual the opportunity to take a far greater degree of control over her or his own workday.

What's in it for you? A present with more control over what you do from hour to hour and a future that is more secure. Not bad for starters.

NEXT WEEK: OK . . . but what are you expected to do exactly?

WIIFM 2

All righty, about the actual mechanics of this Quality First process . . .

It was mentioned last time that the answer to WIIFM (What's in it for me?) with regards to the Quality First process is, "A present with more control over what you do from hour to hour and a future that is more secure."

How's that going to happen and what do you have to do?

The centerpiece of all the various quality-related efforts that will be going on simultaneously in the months (and years) to come will be the quality teams. There will be about 60 or 70 teams, with most teams consisting of 8–10 folks from the Insurance Center plus two folks from IC's partners, the Applications & Solutions Team.

As was mentioned in the previous *WIIFM* message, membership on a quality team is nonvoluntary. That's based on the belief that everyone knows something that no one else knows. Everyone has insights that no one else has. Everyone on the payroll is a thinking adult.

If senior management believed anything less about any individual, why on earth would that person be kept on the payroll?

But, back to the point at hand . . .

The quality teams will meet on a regular basis (probably weekly) to discuss how to improve whatever it is they do. And they'll have the power to pursue ideas and make decisions. Happily, there will be a generous program of recognition, gratitude, and celebration to respond to the accomplishments of the teams.

The team leaders will be trained in advance and there will be an increasing number of classes available to help everyone become better and better at determining appropriate improvements and putting them into action.

One great benefit is that when you have more control over what happens from hour to hour in your own life, your life inevitably becomes a better one.

What's in it for you? A happier you, most likely. And a stronger company of which you can be justly very proud.

NEXT WEEK: Besides the teams, what else is going on?

WIIFM 3

Welcome back . . . to the third *WIIFM* message.

The quality teams are the centerpiece of the Quality First effort and they are the vehicle by which every person in both the Insurance Center and the Applications & Solutions Team will be enrolled in the effort to continually improve the organization.

But what else is there? And why are we going to all this bother anyway?

First question first. The strategic planning effort that began early in the year and resulted in the company's mission statement and the specific projects that will make it possible to achieve those goals paved the way for the Quality First process and will continue to be a rich source of ideas and guidance.

Throughout the company, there will be a number of efforts to analyze the processes that are currently in use and that define what we accept as the "right things to do." The efforts in the Customer Service Department, New Business, and Underwriting that are being assisted by outside consultants are examples of that sort of program.

The recent round of intense leadership training for the supervisors and above (including all quality team leaders) also helped set the stage for the quality process. In addition, quality team leaders will be receiving a day and a half of training.

Various programs of communications and training and recognition will all help to shape and support Quality First.

And the quality teams will be the birthplaces of all manner of improvement efforts.

All of this activity will have a common objective: to improve the products and services that the members of the Insurance Center and its partner, the Applications & Solutions Team, offer to the insureds, to each other, and to our corporate partners and owners (including, of course, the shareholders).

WIIFM? A perfectly valid question.

The answer: A better, stronger, more competitive organization and a better work environment to step into each morning.

Quality First . . . Our ticket to the future. Welcome aboard.

An Invitation to Change

Quality teams were designed as the catalyst for change, and this message invites every employee to become involved. It underscores matching authority with responsibility:

It is a cliché to say that change is inevitable or that the one thing we can count on is change—in our lives, in our jobs, in anything we do. That does not, however, mean that any of us need live in the midst of chaos.

The trick is to be a player in what happens to us. There will be change that we can't control or that we don't even get asked about in advance. That needs to be accepted or, if it is truly a change we can't live with, we need to make a major shift in our lives.

The large majority of time, however, the healthiest response is to focus on what we can control—and change. The Quality First process here at the Insurance Center is an example of the kind of opportunity that makes it possible for anyone on the payroll to have some control over how she or he spends large portions of the day.

Do you think that what you are doing was invented by some troll years ago? Change it. Work with the folks on your quality team and with your quality team leader and change it. Feel like you have no power? Exercise some by developing a quality idea and then working with others to get it implemented. Want to be seen as an active participant in your own life? Define a better way to do something and help make your new way "the way we do things around here . . . until we think of an even better way."

Change will happen. Why not make it change that you think is a good idea?

Pam Walsh's "Unofficial Tips to Quality"

One of the most successful quality team leaders at the Insurance Center made up a list, during Quality Year 1, for the other quality team leaders in her department (Accounting). The CQO spotted the list and published the tips—one at a time—in five consecutive quality newsletters. Pam had some credibility: the quality team she led, the ExcelErs, was the first team to make it to Bronze on the strength of 10 separate ideas, and at the time she wrote the list, her team had more certified quality ideas than any other team in the company.

1. **What bugs me about my job?** That's one way we got started. One team member complained about a box of spoiled checks that she stored under her desk, cramping her leg room. Why was she keeping them? Because we always had. Was it necessary? No. Not a huge thing, but it made her more comfortable and eliminated a box of stuff.

2. **The file that went nowhere.** . . Figure out how things really work. One process we looked at had been designed for North Dallas to mirror the North Richland Hills process. Only problem was that— due to differences in the way the bank systems work—one step was literally sending a file into the North Dallas bank that went nowhere . . . a daily job function that had no purpose.

3. **Taking a close look.** . . Accounts Payable—a pretty straightforward process, right? You pay the bills. But there would be glitches. We invited members from two other teams for cake and flow-charting and, after covering the walls with white paper, we defined nine major functions of the process of cutting one check or a batch of 200 checks, with eight different people involved in the process. We documented it, analyzed it, laughed at it, and then eliminated two of the steps as being totally redundant and unnecessary.

4. **It's an attitude, not just a process.** I think it's important to remember that the team meeting time is not the only time when you "do quality." Quality needs to be part of how we think—constantly challenging ourselves to make things smarter, easier, faster, better. One of the ways we've done this is to congratulate team members for every idea and input. We don't wait for the next team meeting to bounce ideas off of each other. Some of our ideas have come as one of us is working on something, has a brainstorm, calls another team member and plays the "what," "why," "how," "why not" game.

5. **Remember that group project in high school.** You know, where you and I did all the work and those other group members just sailed along to get the A. Sometimes, it can feel that way on

a quality team—that some members aren't contributing or pulling their weight. But the important thing to remember is that results—the A or, in this case, the team making Gold—are what count. If you get caught up in who did what on a team, then you lose sight of the goal and have a lot less fun.

We Haven't Got Time

A frequent complaint made by quality teams had to do with time. This message was written to try to address some of those concerns—and to chide some of the managers:

Perhaps the most common lament—or excuse—voiced by quality team leaders (or the folks they work for) is that "We haven't got time for all those meetings."

Remember the TV ad for a motor oil in which the key line was, "You can pay me now or you can pay me later"? Well, the same idea applies to this notion that, "We haven't got time to change; we're too busy doing it the old way."

Just as sticking with the old oil eventually reduces the ability of an engine to function efficiently and may even lead to a complete breakdown, so too with an insistence on using old, "proven" methods. What worked yesterday (or last year) may well have been the best option then, but times and opportunities and tools all constantly change. If any piece of an organization is ignoring the input of its own people in a constant reevaluation of its work processes because they "don't have the time" (a statement frequently accompanied by an explicit belief that the senior management team of the unit knows best anyway), it is condemning itself to mediocrity.

By refusing to make the investment in time necessary to gather, explore, and implement ideas from people at all levels, the unit ensures that it will always be limited to being "good enough." But it will never excel. The time needed to participate in a quality effort is an investment, not a cost. Pay now or pay later . . . and later costs a whole lot more.

Broadcasting an Update

At the end of the fourth year of Quality First, John Fynn of the Quality Department put together the following as part of the annual discussion of "How are we doing? What do we need to change? Is this still a good idea?":

A few points that always seem to be left out of the conversation when discussing the merits and benefits of the Quality First process . . .
The Quality First process:

1. Encourages participation at every level in the improvement of our processes. (Everyone can participate in the improvement of our company regardless of their position or job description.)

2. Fosters the development of future leaders. (Team leaders acquire experience in team management, written and verbal communication skills, conflict resolution, measurement applications and, basically, "how to get something done.")

3. Encourages ownership of one's job. (An individual is responsible for the effectiveness and efficiency of his or her job and can make changes to improve it.)

4. Nurtures teamwork and cooperation. (Teams experience the productive atmosphere and bonding effect of working together and focusing on common goals.)

5. Increases an individual's awareness of the positive effect he or she can have on the company.

6. Provides a platform for appreciation and recognition of accomplishments. (Recognition ceremonies are a convenient opportunity to say "thank you" and "keep up the good work.")

7. Widens the pool of potential improvements to include input from all associates. (Ideas and suggestions are not limited to a few selected individuals, but are generated from all areas and levels within the company.)

8. Increases the scope of an individual's understanding of processes and "how things are done." (Through the process of implementation of an idea and the interaction between teams and departments, individuals are exposed to more company processes and workflows.)

9. Encourages individual accountability and responsibility. ("I can improve or enhance my personal job responsibilities and processes, which will positively impact my area, my department, and the company.")

10. Increases the awareness of measurement by emphasizing the cost-saving and/or time-saving potential of every idea. (Everyone realizes the financial impact even a small change can have over a period of time and how those small changes can add up to substantial cost savings for the company.)

11. Creates a healthy work environment conducive to creativity and innovation. (Employees who are comfortable and de-stressed are more capable of creative thought processes.)

12. Helps to develop communication skills. (Teams and team leaders gain experience in written and verbal skills.)

13. Emphasizes the importance of our customers' needs. (Teams consider the effects ideas will have on customers, internally and externally.)

Mission, Quality, and Pie-in-the-Face?

As an example of what a company with a thriving CQP effort can feel like, consider the following story sent out to Insurance Center employees after a successful, if a bit nonstandard, food drive for a local charity:

Phil's mantra: "Mission, Quality, and Culture. Mission is what we do, Quality is how we do it, Culture is how we work together to get it done."

In case you've ever wondered why a company that deals in such a serious, life-impacting business as we do and that has such high work expectations for everyone on the payroll can afford to "take the time" to do things like shove pies in the faces of three—well, actually, four—executives, the answer lies in that definition of "culture" and the fact that "culture" is mentioned in the same breath with "mission" and "quality."

We cannot be a company of strangers. We cannot be a collection of people with no feelings for, or opinions about, each other. If we are going to build up, and then keep strengthening, the mutual trust that is so important if we are going to get better, we need to share good moments and to all feel like we are working with folks about whom it is easy to have some positive feelings. We need to have some fun together.

Culture is not a result solely of events like last Thursday's Pie-Throwing. It is also a result of individual acts such as saying "Good morning/afternoon" when we pass someone in the hallway or congratulating someone when they come up with a quality idea. And it is the result of a lot of one-at-a-time acts of leadership at all levels.

Mission, quality, culture. Blended together, they make it possible to continue this incredible run to the top that we have experienced over the last four years.

And the bonus? The Community Enrichment Center food drive that was topped off by the Pie-Throwing resulted in *16 tons of food* being delivered to the CEC Food Bank. Incidentally, that will keep them going for about two weeks.

What Exactly Is a Culture Shift?

Later that same year, this message was published to all associates to congratulate them on their contributions. Talking about corporate culture is second nature at the Insurance Center:

Over the last 10 years or more, one of the hot topics in the world of business has been company culture and, more specifically, culture shifts within an organization. The problem is that there has been far more in the way of academic chatter than there has been in the way of actual examples.

Well, we at the UICI Insurance Center are currently living through a good example of a culture shift.

It is fair to say that, prior to the initiation of the Quality First process, a frequent response to finding a problem of some sort in the company's procedures was to say, "Somebody should do something about that."

After 5000 certified quality ideas, it is now fair to say that when a problem of some sort in the company's procedures is discovered, the most frequent response is, "We need to do something about that; we can fix that with a quality idea."

That is what the academics call a "culture shift."

The impact of the Complete Quality Process on the corporate culture of the UICI Insurance Center came about as a result of common vision and hard work. Employees were able to understand—without any "quality jargon" getting in the way—the goal of the effort and how they could contribute, thanks to a barrage of messages—written, spoken, and behavioral. After five years, the results clearly indicate that the message was received.

10 | Now What?

It's axiomatic that each Complete Quality Process has similarities to other efforts in other organizations, but that each process will soon take on unique aspects. Everything—from an organization's previous experiences with various improvement schemes to the depth of commitment (active, obvious, informed) by senior executives to the willingness and ability of the Quality Department to make adjustments—will impact exactly how quickly and how effectively the CQP principles play out. What stays the same is that each process has to address the seven components examined in this book: top management commitment, leadership, 100 percent employee involvement (with a structure), measurement, training, recognition, and communications. And once a CQP is up and running, each process will have to find ways to grow and change. For a process that calls for change on the part of every person and unit in the organization to not itself be open to change would give new meaning to the word *hypocrisy*.

The Chief Quality Officer and the Quality Department have the responsibility of keeping a Complete Quality Process fresh. Any of the details can change—from the definition of terms to the number of certified ideas needed to reach certain levels of recognition to how ideas are reviewed—so long as the goal of quality improvement is realized. One of the CQO's more important jobs is to work with the other senior managers and keep them committed to the process. This will require listening—a lot. He or she will have to know when to teach, when to lead, and when to say, "Good idea, we can make that change."

And it is impossible to overstate the importance of the quality team leaders. They are trained in how to measure and document the impact of an idea; it is their responsibility to repeatedly ask team members for ideas on how to improve things; and they use the quality idea tracking program and database to communicate with the Quality Department. In a sense, these quality team leaders do take on responsibilities in addition to their "normal" jobs, and the organization has to encourage and support them in their role in every way possible.

Remember the question, "What's in it for me?" For quality team leaders, the answer is "a lot." Without exception, quality team leaders find the position a marvelous opportunity to test their abilities as leaders—in an environment in which almost everyone is pulling for their success and mentors are available in their own department, in the Quality Department, and in the Training Department. The experience—and exposure to senior management—that quality team leaders get accelerates their professional growth.

In addition, everyone involved in a CQP experiences personal growth. Quality is the transferable job skill of the twenty-first century. At a time when government statisticians (while holding on to their own jobs) tell us that we will all switch jobs and careers several times, being open to change, knowing how to initiate change, knowing the value of customers . . . all of these are skills that know no boundaries.

A book on a CQP doesn't have a natural close because any CQP (to include the one at the UICI Insurance Center) is a living reflection of the organization using it to improve itself. The following from the Quality Department at the UICI Insurance Center, however, contains a heartfelt wish for the reader's future success. This Christmas greeting is sent to the associates annually—with minor changes each year, of course:

WE WISH YOU A QUALITY CHRISTMAS

From the Quality Department, these wishes to everyone:

- May each day of your holiday be better than the one before (what we call "continual improvement").

- May everyone be thrilled with what you give them for Christmas (what we call "customer satisfaction").

- May the love you share with your family be strengthened (what we call "building partnerships").

- May everything you plan happen just like you plan it (what we call "error-free execution").

- May the entire time be happy and blessed for each and every one of you (what we call "happy and blessed for each and every one of you").

A The Spirit of Quality in America

by Pat Townsend

Quality. Leadership. Democracy. God-centered religions, including Judaism, Islam, and Christianity. These four concepts, these four ways of thinking about how to conduct ourselves as we journey through the many phases of our lives, have much in common . . . common ground that helps to explain why a commitment to Quality does indeed contribute significantly to building a stronger America.

For instance, at the core of each of these is a belief in the value of the individual—and it is that wholehearted acceptance of the worth of each person that sets these four concepts apart from their lesser competitors for our time and energy.

I'll start with Quality. The willingness to believe—and, essentially, to bet on—the idea that every single person has potential, that each and every person can, to some degree, be creative and contribute to the improvement of the whole, is what sets Quality apart from Productivity.

And, too, the belief that each individual deserves to be given respect and deserves to be given the opportunity to be placed in an environment that makes it possible for him or her to self-actualize in the process of completing their job is what makes Leadership so much more effective than Management.

Central to a Democracy is the concept of "one person, one vote—and all votes have equal value." It is that practical demonstration of the core belief supporting a Democracy, the belief in the importance of each and every citizen, that makes Democracies so far superior to

---

This paper was presented at the 2002 Texas Quality Foundation annual conference.

their autocratic adversaries—superior as places to live, superior as places to raise families, and superior as places to do business.

Fourth, it is the idea that each person has an equal chance at eternal happiness, no matter their material circumstances, that defines the major religions and sets them apart from the ego-centric, often fanatical groups that sometimes usurp their names. Not every group that claims to be part of a religion is truly religious—just remember all those Communist countries that proclaimed themselves to be "people's democracies" when democratic practices were nowhere in view.

It is no accident that no particularly useful ideas in the interrelated areas of Quality and Leadership have come out of countries whose people suffer under totalitarian rule or which are dominated by false religions. If those with power do not accept the fact that there is talent and the ability to think and to be creative at every level of their organization or society, there will be no sustained improvement, there will be no Quality Movement—there will be only the occasional examples thrust forward by the very brave.

That Quality has already helped to make America strong will come as no surprise to the people in this room. But has anyone outside of the Quality Community noticed that the prolonged economic boom and continual increases in productivity that have been amazing analysts for years began when the Baldrige became a part of the business landscape in America, complete with companies teaching each other?

The Baldrige and its approach to Quality reflect the nature of America—allowing us the freedom to determine details and the freedom to determine how to actually complete the trip from here to there; freedoms we have long enjoyed in America. The Deming Prize in Japan reflects the nature of Japan, where because of the population density and the scarcity of natural resources, there was a perceived need for following tightly defined rules, for keeping everyone inside the lines. Europe's ISO reflects the nature of an emerging—and merging—Europe with its great need to make things fit across rapidly disappearing borders. But note that it is the Baldrige, it is the American approach to life and business that has become the worldwide template for quality efforts and that the Baldrige has clones all over the world and that no nation has ever tried to adapt the Deming. Note too that ISO continues to be an uncomfortable fit in the U.S. and is now being recognized more and more as an acceptable step along the way to Quality and perhaps even the Baldrige, rather than being an end in itself.

Recognizing the links between Quality, Leadership, Democracy, and the major religions invites us to do a bit of benchmarking and, thus, speed up our own development in some areas of our business efforts.

For instance, when the Great American experiment in Democracy began late in the 18th century, the question was asked, "Who should we allow to vote—and, thus, to participate?" Phrasing the question that way led the Founding Fathers to the decision to exclude one whole gender and one whole race. It took about 150 years, a long and bloody war, and a couple of constitutional amendments but America did get it straightened out. Here, in the 21st Century, whether we are starting a new Quality effort or reinvigorating a current Quality process, there is no reason to follow the 18th century example and ask, "Who should we allow to participate?" We can skip straight ahead to the 21st century example and ask, "Who can we afford to leave out?" The answer is "Nobody." Welcome to 100% Employee Involvement!

But be warned. Not everyone will participate at every moment. Not everyone answers the invitation to take part—not in Democracies, not in religions, not in response to Leadership, and not in Quality. But the invitation must be extended, the assumption must be made that every individual has something to contribute to the whole. That belief is the foundation of a Quality process, just as it is the foundation that makes America strong, that makes all Democracies strong, that gives well-led organizations of any type a huge advantage, and that makes true religions credible and attractive.

Just as citizens of a Democracy make the best employees of a Quality-seeking company, the reverse is also true. People who are treated with respect in their workplace—where they spend so much time—go back out into the surrounding world more confident of their worth, more willing to be active in other areas of their lives. No one can be involved in an active Quality effort at work and then just leave it there when they go home. They want to know why others aren't providing the same level of service that they strive so hard to offer to their customers and they want to know where to go with their ideas for improvements both in businesses and in government operations at any level. A person who is invited and welcomed into a corporate Quality effort becomes a more active citizen—and that's just one more way that Quality helps to build a stronger and better America.

Please note that when I speak of Quality, I have in mind the sort of effort envisioned by the creators of the Baldrige—one which is significantly different from the limited but sometimes more popular, consultant-driven approaches that litter the landscape today. I am not saying that efforts such as ISO or Six Sigma or the like do not have merit because they most surely do have great merit. What needs to be pointed out and understood, however, is that these methodologies are sub-sets of a complete quality process and that they are too often designed to insure that an organization reaches and maintains agreed-to minimums. A true Quality process, a well-conceived Baldrige or Quality Texas effort, instead invites you as a person and invites you as an organization to reach for your maximum achievement levels—and then to get better again.

It is that sort of continual drive, of always looking to—and expecting to—build one success upon another, that is the hallmark of Quality and it is how Quality helps to build a stronger America . . . now and in the years to come.

B Love and Leadership

by Pat Townsend

The English language, so rich in variety that there is a recognized network of words for expressing virtually every nuance of any central concept, has been strangely abused in one key area—love. We have come to limit its meaning, on the personal level, to two instances—family and sex. We are uncomfortable, for instance, to hear of one man loving another, or of a married person admitting love for a member of the opposite sex other than their spouse.

Yet there are many manifestations of love, and one of the greatest is good leadership. We acknowledge this with statements such as "he really loves his men" or "they really love him," but we rarely look past the clichés. Love and leadership are not synonymous terms, but since leadership is a form of love, our knowledge and experience of the root concept can provide us with useful insights into leadership.

Perhaps the most obvious thing that leadership and love have in common is the act of caring about the welfare of others—an act that is central to both. One's love for another implies caring for the well-being, physical and mental, of the other. Conversely, a failure to notice, or to obviously care about, a decline in the quality of someone's state of existence is taken as proof that "you don't love me anymore." In the parallel case, if the "led" perceive that their leader doesn't care about the fact that, for example, their food is bad and getting worse, he will quickly be adjudged a poor leader. This idea is

This article first appeared in *The Marine Corps Gazette* in February 1982. It received a Distinguished Performance Award from the Marine Corps Combat Correspondents Association later that year. It was written by then-Major Pat Townsend.

formalized by the fact that taking care of the troops is considered second in importance only to the accomplishment of the mission.

It is that ordering, more than anything else, that makes the words love and leadership nonsynonymous.

Marine, the biography of Chesty Puller, provides a classic example of the close tie between love and leadership. Anyone who reads *Marine* and ignores the tender love letters to his wife, written from combat, misses the point of the book and of the man. Chesty Puller loved his men and they him, just as truly and as fiercely as he loved his wife and family. His great capacity for love enhanced immeasurably his abilities as a leader.

A person who would call himself, or herself, a leader of Marines must be capable of love, of allowing themselves to be loved, and of understanding the awesome responsibilities incurred when one seeks and accepts the love of others. To love someone is to make a commitment to them, a promise to work hard to better them and to better yourself. It is not a pledge to nag them until they finally shape up but rather a promise to work with them towards a mutual goal, a higher state.

This is not to say that I am advocating a utopian democracy for the Corps in which leaders and followers somehow merge into one happy, loving homogeneous group. Remember, I said the words are not synonymous. Nor is it to say a person in a leadership position who loves the people assigned to his responsibility will automatically be a great leader. However, without the ability to love, he will not be a great, and perhaps not even a good, leader. The technical knowledge, the courage, the personal integrity so often discussed are definitely necessary. Love though is what makes it work; it is what makes the followers willingly accept the technical knowledge and treat the courage and personal integrity as something to emulate rather than just applaud.

The relationship between the leader and the follower(s) is most closely analogous to that between parent and child. The good parent listens to his child and considers both the child's desires and abilities along with outside demands and personal responsibilities before making a decision. Whenever possible, that decision is explained to the child. Also, the good parent will strive to set a good example for the child.

In both love and leadership, perception is frequently as important as reality. If someone is perceived as being a good leader or of loving, then the recipient of that leadership or love will normally react by willingly following or returning the love. The importance of ensuring that the object of the leadership or love is aware of outward signs that are taken as positive evidence of love or leadership increases as the distance—both physical and organizational—between the leader and the follower(s), the lover and the loved one(s), increases. The possibility of successfully faking it, of making the perception different than the reality, also increases as the distance grows.

A grandparent, for instance, is perceived as loving by a grandchild if he or she is careful to never miss a birthday or Christmas. Likewise, troops rarely see their commanding general and few ever actually talk with him. Yet every Marine will offer an opinion about his general, will tell you whether he will happily follow him and give that extra effort. This assessment, largely emotional, which will translate itself into tangible performance, is based on a combination of the reputation that the general built for himself on the way up, on the individual Marine's knowledge/perception of his performance in his current job as commanding general, and on the individual Marine's perception of how well the command is "taking care" of him.

In point of fact, the commanding general may be doing very little himself to see that his troops' physical and mental welfare is being attended to. He may not even be "setting the tone" but rather be simply blessed, accidentally or intentionally, with a good staff. Similarly, a child will profess his love for both grandparents—since both have been signing the cards that came with the gifts. Yet it's possible that left to his own devices, grandpa might never admit that he has grandchildren, let alone remember their birthdays.

A historical example is offered by Napoleon. His men loved him as proved by their statements and their actions. Yet Napoleon's cavalier attitude towards them was summed up in his claim that had "an income of 20,000 men a month to spend." His troops didn't know his opinion of them. They knew only that he had led them to glory and satisfied both physical and mental needs and desires.

The reverse is also possible. A leader may be an extremely talented technician with a deep love for his people, but if that talent and that feeling are not made known to the Marines he would lead, he may as well not have them. Without a capable staff, the filter through which the enlisted and the majority of the officers see their commanding general, the fruits of his knowledge and love will be minimal.

Looking again at the parallel case of the lover and the loved ones. A grandmother's deep love for her grandchildren will not be recognized if she is unable to acknowledge special occasions, can never visit, and/or is being presented in a bad light by her "staff," grandpa, parents, and other relatives.

As the distance is decreased, the concepts of love and leadership become more obviously intertwined. A platoon commander, while laying out the groundwork for the reputation that will follow him throughout his career, must truly love his men if he wishes to be known as a good leader. If he brings technical expertise and ambition, but no warmth, to his position, his troops will return his investment in like currency. They will do precisely what he says, but will not give the extra effort that is the mark of the well-led.

Another point of similarity is the willingness to forgive that is common to both loving relationships and to leading-led relationships. Not only will on-going faults be overlooked or compensated for, mistakes will be tolerated and not held against the lover. So too with the leader whose men are returning the love/leadership they perceive as being offered freely to them. Many a young lieutenant has been saved because the men under his command "covered for him." It was no accident, just as it was no accident when adjacent units chose not to cover for their lieutenants. In the former case, love is being returned in full.

As these young officers climb through the ranks and become more and more distant from the troops, they will still have a group of officers and men with whom they must deal on a person-to-person basis. At the highest levels, this will be the general's staff. As I mentioned above, success at that level will be a combination of the reputation earned, the common perception of his competence, and the perception, as seen through the filter of his staff, of his love for his troops. As long as the people who make up his staff feel loved, they will pass on to the lower levels that they too are truly loved. This explains, of course, how Napoleon could be so loose with his "income" of men and yet be loved by them. He did ensure that his staff felt loved and appreciated and so they conveyed their feelings towards him to the common soldier.

What makes all of this threatening to many officers, young and old, is that it involves taking a rather large chance for, unfortunately, to just love your troops won't be enough. Just as the object of one's romantic love may not always be swept off her feet on schedule, so too in a leading-led relationship. As a result, you might find yourself a victim of unrequited love on a grand scale. Love is what makes it work, and the loved and the well-led will overlook and/or compensate for some weaknesses, but there must be some substance, some technical knowledge, to hang onto. Conversely, technical substance by itself will ensure meeting minimum objectives and, if that's all you have, will just as surely doom you to having to settle for minimum performance.

It is the leader who combines a deep love, an ability to love and be loved, with technical knowledge and dedication who will rise to the top. It is the leader who makes an active effort to ensure the physical and mental welfare of those placed under his responsibility and whose people know it—the leader who blends the emotional and rational elements—who is the stuff that legends are made of.

To establish both the similarities and the differences, compare the two lists below. First are the principles of leadership as laid out in the *Guidebook for Marines*. Next are the analogous "principles of love." Just as adherence to the principles of leadership—a task made impossible if the leader does not love his people (see #6 and #11 in particular)—promises success in the military, so too would adherence to their counterparts come close to guaranteeing a successful personal relationship.

Principles of Leadership

1. Take responsibility for your actions and the actions of your Marines. Use responsibility with judgment, tact, and initiative. Be loyal, be dependable.

2. Know yourself and seek self-improvement. Evaluate yourself. Be honest with yourself about yourself.

3. Set the example.

4. Develop your subordinates.

5. Ensure that a job is understood, then supervise it and carry it through to completion.

6. Know your men and look after their welfare. Share problems but don't pry.

7. Every man should be kept informed.

8. Set goals you can reach.

9. Make sound and timely decisions.

10. Know your job.

11. Teamwork.

Principles of Love

1. Take responsibility for your actions and share the responsibility, if appropriate and welcome, for your loved one's actions. Treat your loved one with judgment and tact. Be loyal and dependable.

2. Know yourself and seek self-improvement so that your "team" can grow. Don't lie to yourself about yourself or your loved one.

3. Don't make demands that you wouldn't want made of you.

4. Using tact and judgment, offer to take part in your loved one's growth and invite them to be part of yours.

5. Ensure that any requests that you make that are important to you are correctly understood.

6. Know your loved one's needs and wants and be concerned about their physical and mental welfare. Ensure that they know that you are available to share any problem, while still allowing privacy.

7. Always communicate. If something is important enough to you that it affects your behavior, tell your loved one about it.

8. Be realistic in your expectations. You are not going to be in Shangri-la every day.

9. Make the necessary decisions as well and responsively as you can.

10. Know the "mechanical" aspects of your relationship, the job of building and nurturing a solid relationship.

11. Share with and work with your loved one towards agreed goals.

The Anatomy of
a Dictaphone
by Lillian S. Murphy

Top credit goes to Thomas Edison, the miracle man. He was the first to record the human voice. With the aid of paraffin and beeswax, Alexander Graham Bell improved on the recording and reproduction. Luckily for the business world, Dictaphone Corp. recognized its endless transcription possibilities and their "Writing Out Loud" was born.

Now, I'm a Dictaphone operator and a good one. I've been in the business a long time. Oddly enough, some of the dictators I've worked for are absolutely socially perfect, yet their dictation has made many a transcriber weep all the way to the personnel office.

Actually, dictating is simple enough. It's merely a matter of consideration—consideration for the operator, that is. When we stop to think that today's typing prices work out at about $3.31 for even the shortest letter, then obviously, business expenses can no longer be swept under the rug.

Take a small office, for instance. Here, the secretary has only to put her boss straight regarding any transcription difficulties, and they're off to a good start. Not so when it comes to a larger company, especially one which sports its own stenographic pool. It does seem that rarely is there an opportunity for the hard-working transcriber to be heard at any of the office manager's meetings.

Ironically, many big concerns proudly fly their suggestion boxes like a banner, little appreciating that it takes sheer guts for an employee to put her name to a totally bold or strong suggestion. Here, the company is definitely the loser, for if they could only get a sneak preview of behind-the-scenes activities from the transcriber's angle, much time and subsequent expense could be saved.

This article was originally printed in the May 1975 issue of *Supervision* magazine.

Very often, verbal pleas for transcribing improvements are actually suggested to the supervisor of the department, but if no promising changes are in the offing, after a time, the operator will stop caring. After all, it's no skin off her nose. If time is lost through a dictator not making his correspondence absolutely clear, for instance, if he's chewing while talking or turning his head away from the mike, etc., then ultimately, it's the company who suffers the loss.

Would you believe one of the best dictators I've had the pleasure to transcribe from was doing his dictation in the comfort of his own home. This is fine with me. However, when his wife started out with the vacuum cleaner at the opposite end of the room, no harm was done, but as she gradually got nearer and nearer until she was actually vacuuming around the chair he was sitting in, the volume of the vacuum cleaner completely drowned out every word of his dictation. And then he registered surprise when he was told that that particular portion of his dictation could not be transcribed.

It's par for the course that most rules set down by many businesses are mostly launched by individuals who actually never come anywhere near handling or performing the routine duties for which they lay down the laws. As an experiment, offer to let a transcription operator openly voice her opinion about her own working domain in your company. Chances are, you may be in for some big surprises.

After all, it's a foregone conclusion that once the operator is aware of the company's needs and the dictator learns of the transcriber's needs, everything should magically and smoothly coincide.

Among the majority of common dictating difficulties lurks the busy dictator who merely drops the word "correction" for good measure. However, in actual fact, he has not gone back over the tape to erase his mistake or whatever his system is for making or marking corrections. Now, a real eggshell-willed girl will probably mask her ruffled feathers, but another type of operator might just go for a walk to the ladies room to cool off. The company will never know the time and paper lost in righting a wrong that was so simple it should never have been allowed to slip by in the first place.

Large companies often have production sheets, and this is more tormenting to the dictaphone operator than any other department. One cannot possibly gauge the production of a diligent operator coping with a dictator who, for instance, might be dictating columns of figures. If he says "$9" and waits, that's what she'll type. Then maybe he'll add the word "and" before completing "25 cents." Production is held up while corrections of this nature are adjusted, but it's unfair to record the dictaphone operator's turnout when things of this nature prevent a steady flow of uninterrupted work.

Essential articulation often appears elusive—ask any dictaphone operator—but it often has a way of disappearing altogether when the person dictating decides that they can't possibly last out until the next work break. Thus, to the sinking chagrin of the conscientious operator, obvious indications of chewing gum, pipe puffing, or other pleasures of the jaw accompany the correspondence.

Spelling technical and unusually difficult words is another bugbear, and while an operator would much prefer to fly to a dictionary if the dictator is making a mad and incorrect guess, nevertheless, it will save much time and money, to say nothing of frustration, if this assistance can be provided.

A little verbal bouquet is never amiss; whether it's to an individual or the typing pool in general. As Mark Twain aptly remarked, "On a good compliment, I can go two months." Ask any transcriber to compare how many complaints she can offset against the number of praises her department receives. It's a well-known fact that a happy atmosphere makes for considerably more production than a clouded one, any day of the week. In other words, it's nice to know when you're doing right as well as when you're doing wrong.

Of course, there will be complaints occasionally. The man who doesn't make mistakes doesn't do any work—or the woman either, for that matter. However, these should be tackled as pleasantly as possible for the sake of everyone's feelings.

It need not be added that coughing into the mike is strictly taboo. However, you wouldn't believe how many dictators seem to find a certain satisfaction when they're straining someone's eardrum. Or so it would appear.

When extra copies of correspondence are required, naturally, they have to be directed at the end of the material, so it's futile to waste the operator's time in her making extra notes when these are called for at the beginning of the communication. Just saying how many copies are needed at the start is sufficient and giving their destination at the end is simple. Living in this convenient photocopy age is terrific, but photocopy paper is expensive when its use so easily can be avoided by carefully arranging of correspondence before the dictation is started. Misunderstood instructions are always expensive.

And what about the happy-go-lucky individual who accumulates his correspondence all week and then hogs the dictaphone, exercising his melodious voice with a stream of complicated last-minute rush jobs late on Friday afternoon. Needless to say, his lack of consideration will go down in at least one person's estimation.

Of course, the verbal communication between dictator and transcriber is double-edged, and there naturally will be times when, despite your perfect recordings, irritating errors will creep up on the completed material. It would be so great if any corrections could be made on a carbon copy where it wouldn't matter, but often, they not only are made on the original, but they also are decorated in colored ballpoint making it impossible for the operator to fix the correction without retyping. Very often, a lead pencil would suffice if the original letter itself is to be altered.

For the most part, it can be appreciated that the efficiency of your transcription operator is precisely a reflection of your careful dictation. Consequently, if you enjoy a merry liquid lunch and your dictation comes over slightly slurred, to say the least, while you yourself may be feeling no pain, it's hardly fair to let the typist know in no uncertain terms that your completed material is unrecognizable.

Even when a business operation runs on square wheels, there will certainly be occasions when an operator simply has to stay late to complete an important piece of transcribing. A word of thanks is all that is required here, but if it does run into a fair portion of time, it would be nice to give the equivalent time off at some convenient later date.

Of course, there's one in every outfit—the chap who just doesn't enunciate—and wouldn't believe it if you told him so. Undoubtedly excelling in almost every other facet of his job performance, one weakness he fails to admit even to himself might be in the concept of clear enunciation. This, then, could be a classic example of Abd-el-Kadir who is reported to have said, "It is with a word as with an arrow—once let it loose, and it does not return."

The obvious strain of a weary dictaphone typist in her valiant efforts to decipher such a mess can rarely be disguised. If there's a solution to those guilty of this most common problem, a successful way to bridge this gap, I'd like to know, for in all my 40-odd years of transcribing experiences, this is certainly the only dictaphone dilemma I haven't been able to solve.

When the operator and the dictator are aware of each other's needs, everything should then magically and smoothly coincide.

Summary

1. Permit transcription operators to occasionally sit in on office manager's meetings and proffer verbal suggestions.

2. Prevent any distractions being recorded on the tape such as paper rustling, music, coughing, background voices, and noises.

3. Avoid word distortions caused by eating, chewing gum, or pipe puffing.

4. Don't fail to make correction marks.

5. Clear enunciation is essential.

6. Talk in a conversational tone, don't whisper or mumble.

7. Dictate paragraphs and uncommon punctuation.

8. Dictate figures by digits without pausing between dollars and cents.

9. Spell names and unusual words correctly.

10. Whenever possible, give to the transcriber the accompanying correspondence.

References

Crosby, Phil. 1980. *Quality Is Free*. New York: The New American Library, Inc; First Mentor Printing.

Kouzes, James M., and Barry Z. Posner. 1987. *The Leadership Challenge*. San Francisco: Jossey-Bass.

Lopez, Charles E. 1992. "On Quality, the Baldridge, and Disinformation: Michael Spiess Sets the Record Straight." *The Quality Observer*. (January): 10, 12, 16.

Murphy, Lillian S. 1975. "The Anatomy of a Dictaphone." *Supervision* (May): 20-21.

Panko, Ron. 2001. "Stealth Solution." *Best's Review*: (November): 53–62.

Peters, Thomas J. 1986–1994. Various speeches, newsletters, and conversations.

Peters, Thomas J., and Robert H. Waterman. 1982. *In Search of Excellence*. New York: Harper & Row.

Reimann, Curt W., and Harry S. Hertz. 1993. "The Malcolm Baldrige Award & ISO 9000 Registration: Understanding Their Many Important Differences." Gaithersburg, MD: National Institute of Standards and Technology.

"Rethinking Rewards." 1993. *Harvard Business Review* (November–December).

Sandberg, Jared. 2005. "Overcontrolling Bosses Aren't Just Annoying; They're Also Inefficient." *Wall Street Journal* (March 30): B-1.

Steeples, Marion M. 1992. *The Corporate Guide to the Malcolm Baldrige National Quality Award: Proven Strategies for Building Quality into Your Organization*. Milwaukee, WI: ASQC Press/Business One Irwin.

Townsend, Patrick, and Joan Gebhardt. 1986. *Commit to Quality*. New York: John Wiley & Sons.

———. 1992. *Quality in Action: 93 Lessons in Leadership, Participation, and Measurement*. New York: John Wiley & Sons.

———. 1997. *Five-Star Leadership: The Art and Strategy of Creating Leaders at Every Level*. New York: John Wiley & Sons.

———. 1997. *Recognition, Gratitude & Celebration*. Menlo Park, CA: Crisp Publications.

United States Army. 1990. *Military Leadership (FM 22-100).* Washington, D.C.: United States Army.

United States Marine Corps. 1980. *Guidebook for Marines.* Washington, D.C.: United States Marine Corps.

United States Marine Corps. 1990. *Marine Corps Leadership (MCI 7404).* Washington, D.C.: United States Marine Corps.

White, Erin. 2005. "Savviest Job Hunters Research the Cultures of Potential Employers." *Wall Street Journal* (March 29): B-1.

Index

A

accountability, 39
agendas
    for CQP, at UICI Insurance
        Center, 49–50
    for quality committees, 22
American Quality Revolution, 1
Ames Rubber Company, 71
analysts, quality, 66
    role of, 67
authority, 22
    methods for moving up
        corporate level, 39–40
    pushing down, 38–41
authority leadership, 42–43

B

benchmarking, 88, 89–90
bottom line, 7, 12–13
    of recognition programs,
        103

C

capacity for work, 10–12, 13
    at UICI Insurance Center, 15
celebrations, 103–5. *See also*
    recognition programs
change, invitation to, 116

charting, 88
chief quality officers (CQOs),
    24
commitment
    best arguments for, to
        quality, 17–18
    rational, 35–36
    senior leadership and, 43–44
    sustaining, senior
        management and, 29–31
    top management and, 5–6
committees. *See* quality
    committees; Quality
    Steering Committees
    (QSCs); search
    committees
communication, 107–8
    listening down and, 108–9
    receiving messages and,
        109–11
    transmitting messages and,
        109–11
Complete Quality Process
    (CQP), 1
    beginning process of, 2
    components of, 1–2
    financially unstable
        companies and, 5
    finding leaders for, 20–21
    as lifetime process, 4

messages designed to answer "What's in it for me?" and, 112–15
passion vs. system and, 33
pursuing components simultaneously, 3
reasons for not pursuing, 3–4
reasons organizations choose not to adopt, 51–53
recognition programs and, 97–100
results of, at UICI Insurance Center, 94–95
simplicity of, 2–3
Conseco Insurance Company, 15, 16
consumers, power of, 8–10
continual problems, 87–88
contractors, quality teams and, 69
corporate culture, 25, 53, 120, 121–22
CQP. *See* Complete Quality Process (CQP)
creative discontent, 54–55
example of, 135–39
Crosby, Phil, 7
culture, corporate, 25, 53, 120, 121–22
curriculum, for training team leaders, 77–78
customers
capturing and keeping, 10
defining, 73
determining expectations of, 73–74
kinds of disconnect with, 73
cyclical problems, 87

D

delegative leadership, 42, 43
Deming, W. Edwards, 1, 83

dictation, suggestions for giving, 135–39
discontent, creative, 54–55
example of, 135–39
doing "things right" questions, answering, 65

E

emotional commitment, 35–36
emotions, leadership and, 34–35
employees
new, orientation training for, 71–74
temporary, quality teams and, 69
empowerment, 39, 41
examples, setting, 43–44

F

FedEx, 7
Feigenbaum, Armand, 1
focus groups, 51–52
Froedtert Lutheran Memorial Hospital, 105
Fynn, John, 26, 28, 29, 90, 92, 93, 119

G

gifts, for recognition programs, 98–100
gratitude, expressing, 98–100, 103

H

Haig, Alexander, 110
hard-dollar savings, 12–13
Hill, Max, 47, 102
humor, 59–60

I

ideas, quality. *See* quality ideas
inspection, 84. *See also*
    measurement
Insurance Center. *See* UICI
    Insurance Center
ISO standards, 4, 87
IT Departments, involvement
    of, 30

J

Japanese Quality Control
    Circle initiatives, 51–52
job-specific training vs. quality
    training, 79–80
judgment, poor, 4
Juran, Joseph, 1

K

Kilbury, Richard, 40
Kouzes, Jim, 35

L

leaders, of CQP. *See also* team
    leaders
    finding, 20–21
    military veterans and, 24
    qualifications for, 21–23
    search committees and,
        20–21
leadership
    case study of, at UICI
        Insurance Center, 46–47
    defined, 75
    emotions and, 34–35
    management as subset of,
        34–35
    personal, 47
    principles of, 133

priorities of, 42
styles of, 42–43
as subset of love, 43
trust and, 38–41
UICI Insurance Center case
    study of, 46–47
U.S. Marine Corps
    principles of, 41–42
learning, willingness and, 21
Licensing Department, UICI
    Insurance Center, 14
listening down, 108–9
love
    leadership as subset of, 43,
        129–33
    principles of, 134

M

management, as subset of
    leadership, 34–35. *See also*
    senior management
Mao Tse-Tung, 56
Marine Corps. *See* U.S. Marine
    Corps
McConville, Robert, 65
measurement, 83–84
    benchmarking for, 88, 89–90
    charting for, 88
    quality ideas for, 91–94
    rational and emotional
        aspects of, 84
    resistance to, 90–91
    selecting right tool for, 87
    for success, 94–95
    surveys for, 88–89
    types of problems and,
        87–88
    UICI Insurance Center
        approach to, 85–86
messages, transmission of,
    109–11
military veterans, 24

money, making, quality and, 7
Motorola, 4, 79, 87
Murphy, Lillian S., 55
Myhra, Phil, 24–25, 25, 27, 28,
    46, 53, 85, 102, 107

O

orientation training, 71–74
outputs, 11–12
outside vendors, for training
    team leaders, 78–79

P

participation
    100 percent, 49, 51, 52
    UICI Insurance Center case
        study in, 55–60
    on UICI Insurance Center
        quality teams, 49–51
    volunteering and, 49–51
participative leadership, 42, 43
Paul Revere Insurance Group
    PEET program at, 45–46
    Quality Steering committee
        at, 28
PEET (Program for Ensuring
    Everybody's Thanked),
    44–46
periodic problems, 87
personal leadership, 47
Peters, Tom, 1, 33, 34, 44, 71
power, of consumers, 8–10
power sharing, 3
problems, types of, 87–88
processes
    changing, 66
    work, looking at, 63–64
productivity
    vs. quality, 11–12
    as subset of quality, 34

profit, case study of, at UICI
    Insurance Center, 14–16
profits. *See* bottom line
Program for Ensuring
    Everybody's Thanked
    (PEET), 44–46
purists, quality, 53–55
Pym, Jeff, 65

Q

quality
    best arguments for senior
        management for
        commitment to, 17–18
    consumers and, 10
    introducing, to employees,
        111–12
    long-term commitment to,
        43–44
    making money and, 7
    measurement tools for, 87
    not having time and, 118
    by proclamation, 19–20
    vs. productivity, 11–12
    productivity as subset of,
        34
    putting a face on, 19–23
    selecting leaders for, 20–23
    simplicity and difficulty
        of, 5
    spirit of, in America,
        125–28
    unofficial tips to, 116–18
quality analysts, 66
    role of, 67
quality circles, 52
quality committees, 21–22. *See
    also* Quality Steering
        Committees (QSCs);
        search committees
    agenda items for, 22

Quality First process, 28, 105.
See also UICI Insurance
Center
merits and benefits of,
119–20
team leaders and, 47
quality ideas
contract negotiations and,
69
cost savings of, 68–69
defined, 50, 67
sharing of, 67–68
tracking programs for,
91–94
vs. "your job," 69
Quality in Fact, defined,
72–73
Quality in Perception, defined,
72, 73
quality purists, 53–55
Quality Steering Committees
(QSCs). *See also* quality
committees
forming teams and, 76
participation on, 50–51
at Paul Revere Insurance
Group, 28
recognition programs and,
44–46
at UICI Insurance Center,
27–29
quality teams, 81. *See also* team
leaders
contractors and, 69
credit and savings for ideas
and, 68
gaining momentum and,
64–66
intentions of, 67
membership and, 68
naming, 105–6
participation on, 50–51

temporary employees and,
69
at UICI Insurance Center,
49–51, 60–63
quality training, vs. job
training, 79–80

R

rational commitment, 35–36
reception, of messages, 109–11
recognition programs, 44–46.
See also celebrations
bottom line of, 103
gifts for, 98–100
problem of, 101
schedules for, 99, 100
senior management and,
102–3
at UICI Insurance Center,
97–100
resources, 11–12
responsibility, 22, 39
Ritz Carlton, 7, 75

S

Sandberg, Jared, 40
savings. *See also* bottom line
hard-dollar, 12–13
soft-dollar, 13–14
search committees, finding
leaders of CQP and,
20–22. *See also* quality
committees
senior management. *See also*
management
best arguments for
commitment to quality
for, 17–18
commitment and, 5
defining, 30–31

poor judgment and, 4
recognition programs and,
102–3
sustaining commitment to
quality and, 29–31
Six Sigma, 4, 83
soft-dollar savings, 13–14
Soule, Chuck, 33
Spies, Michael, 8
"Spirit of Quality of America,
The" (Townsend), 125–28
statistical process control
(SPC), 83
strategic planning, quality
process and, 29–30
success, measuring, 94–95
suggestion systems, UICI
Insurance Center
example of, 55–60
surveys, 88–89

T

task forces, 87
team leaders. *See also* leaders;
quality teams
guidelines for, 66–70
outside vendors for
training, 78–79
qualifications for, 47
Quality First and, 47
training curriculum for, 77
training for, 69, 76–77
temporary employees, quality
teams and, 69
thank you, saying, 97–99
time, not having, quality and,
118
tips, unofficial, to quality,
116–18
top management. *See* senior
management
Townsend, Pat, 23–24, 125–28

tracking programs, for quality
ideas, 91–94
training, 71
curriculum for, 77
deciding on candidates for,
69, 76–77
orientation, 71–74
quality vs. job, 79–80
at UICI Insurance Center, 80
transcription operators, 135–39
transmission, of messages,
109–11
trust, 36–38
leadership and, 38–41
turnover, employee, 16

U

UICI Insurance Center. *See also*
Quality First process
capacity for work at, 15
case study of leadership at,
46–47
case study of profit at, 14–16
case study of top
management
commitment at, 23–29
celebrations at, 104–5
corporate culture at, 121–22
CQP agenda for, 49–50
Licensing Department of, 14
measurement tools at, 88
orientation training at, 71–72
quality teams at, 49–51,
60–63
quality training at, 80
recognition program at,
97–100
results of CQP at, 94–95
vision statement for, 25–26
workforce turnover at, 16
U.S. Marine Corps, leadership
principles of, 41–42

V

vendors, outside, for training
    team leaders, 78–79
veterans, military, 24
vision statements, 25–26
volunteering, quality
    committees and, 49–51

W

Wallace, John, 7–8
Wallace Company, 7–8
Walsh, Pam, 116–18
Waterman, Bob, 44
Welch, Jack, 4, 33
Wendt, Gary C., 15, 16

"What's in it for me?" (WIIFM),
    messages to answer
    question of, 112–15
Whelan, Candace, 20, 63, 90
White, Erin, 109
WIIFM. *See* "What's in it for
    me?" (WIIFM)
willingness to learn, 20
work, capacity for, 10–12, 13
    at UICI Insurance Center, 15
work processes, looking at,
    63–64
workshops, for CQP, 26–27

X

Xerox, 87

About the Authors

Pat Townsend

An internationally acclaimed author and speaker on the topics of leadership, continual improvement, and recognition, Pat Townsend reentered the corporate world in February 2000 as the Chief Quality Officer for the UICI Insurance Center, an individual health insurance company in the Fort Worth, Texas area. His mission was to be the catalyst for a quality process that actively involved every one of the Insurance Center's employees in the continual improvement of every aspect of the corporation.

He has succeeded in leading the implementation of a Complete Quality Process (CQP), his unique—and uniquely successful—approach to ensuring that an organization's quality effort reaches every aspect of the company and that the organization benefits from the knowledge, ability, and enthusiasm of every person on the payroll. The CQP at the Insurance Center began within eight months of Townsend's arrival and immediately showed impressive bottom-line results.

Townsend had spent the previous dozen years giving keynote presentations and conducting workshops throughout the United States and in Turkey, Brazil, India, Belarus, Sweden, Canada, Finland, and Singapore.

He was a member of the committee that defined and established the Malcolm Baldrige National Quality Award and was an examiner for that award for two years.

Joan Gebhardt

This is the seventh book that Joan Gebhardt has coauthored with Pat Townsend on the overlapping topics of quality, leadership, recognition, and organizational learning. She brings the unique perspective of having always worked in nonmanagement roles—doing everything from decorating eggs for a boutique to being a department secretary at a college.

She has been a member of quality teams such as those described in this book and she authored a Malcolm Baldrige National Quality Award application that led to a site visit in the inaugural year of the award.

Gebhardt designs and codelivers workshops on quality and leadership for senior management teams intent on improvement. Among the countries in which she has taught are India, Singapore, Brazil, Finland, and the United States.

She has a bachelor's degree in history and a lifetime teaching credential from the State of California. She has two sons: Michael, an artist, and Brady, a high-school math teacher and volleyball coach. Gebhardt is an inveterate reader and is also the coauthor of a mystery novel.